SOCRATES ONCE SAID...

ROBERT FORMAN

the Peppertree Press

Sarasota, Florida

In Memoriam

Jack Birchfield, former Assistant Director of the Alumni Association of the University of Michigan, died as this book was going to press. Jack demonstrated in the final days of his life, the same display of dignity, courage and concern for others that exemplified his entire life. His love of family, commitment to his work and unfailing kindness to others served as a model for all who were privileged to know him.

DEDICATION

This book is dedicated to three former colleagues who are no longer with us: Ray Willemain, former alumni director at Northwestern University; Arlie Mucks, former alumni director at the University of Wisconsin and Jerry Tardy former alumni director at Indiana University.

They taught us the value of commitment, camaraderie, love of alma mater, leadership, friendship and self-deprecating humor. They were each in his own way, eloquent spokespersons for the role of alumni in maintaining and enhancing higher education in America.

Of them, Socrates would have said, "Persons are immortal when their thoughts are remembered, their counsel still followed, and thinking of them gives us delight and pleasure."

ACKNOWLEDGMENTS

This modest effort would not have been accomplished if it were not for the support and advice of many people. My wife, Patti, proofread the text in an attempt to prove that I am not illiterate, and constantly reminded me of my procrastination. Jamie Jeremy, alumni director at Western Michigan University, read several aborted earlier attempts and encouraged me to keep trying. Lynn Carver, retired associate alumni director at Northwestern University, tried to instruct me in the essay form, and was kind enough to finally say, "Do it your own way."

Lew Morrisey, retired Director of State Outreach at the University of Michigan, friend and former colleague, read the book from the perspective of a person not directly related to the field of alumni relations. His advice, which I greatly appreciated and followed, proved invaluable.

Joe Small, president of Alumni Holidays International, and Phil Super, president of American Insurance Administrators, agreed to jointly fund this enterprise without first reading the book. I am most grateful for the fact that after reading it, they did not revoke their funding.

In addition, I would like to thank two friends and former Big Ten colleagues, Dan Heinlen, retired president of The Ohio State Alumni Association, and Larry Preo, retired executive director of the Purdue Alumni Association. You will note that on several occasions, I have made a feeble attempt at humor at their expense. My only defense is that we kid people we like and admire. For further proof, note all the people I did not mention.

I also would like to thank two people who once told me, "You should write a book," but that was at a cocktail party and I cannot recall their names.

ROBERT FORMAN 回 V

VI ◉ SOCRATES ONCE SAID

PREFACE

Once during a candid discussion at a Council of Alumni Association Executives (CAAE) meeting, I noted that I had long been impressed with speakers who wove quotes from Greek philosophers into their talks. I admit that I tried to emulate their approach; however, I could never find appropriate quotes. Apparently, neither Socrates nor Plato gave much thought to the field of alumni relations. Since the CAAE discussions focused on ethics, I felt compelled to admit that for years I had been making up Socratic quotes and inserting them in my talks.

This confession was ill advised. From that moment on, my colleagues referred to me as Socrates, not because of my virtue as a philosopher, but because of my confession. On one occasion, my colleagues presented me with a T-shirt with an image of Socrates and my name below as Socrates Forman.

As the executive director of the Alumni Association of the University of Michigan for nearly three decades, I did not learn much Greek philosophy, but I do remember a few things about being an alumni professional.

INTRODUCTION

In my dotage, I have taken to reading essays and memoirs written by folks long dead. When I was a young man, such opinions might have been useful, perhaps giving me some special insight into life's fundamental questions; at this stage, I wonder why I care.

Writers seem eager to advance favorable opinions of themselves. Autobiographies almost always tell of early challenges that the author overcame despite considerable odds. Most often, the problems were not of his or her doing but were caused by others. The author then allows how one can overcome such unfair disadvantages if one only had his or her courage, religious commitment, perseverance and good looks.

Yet I find a fascination in what other people have thought, and when I find that Ralph Waldo Emerson and I have something in common, my own ego is stroked. It is surprising how often one reads something and proudly concludes that the author shares your viewpoints.

I recently read a series of essays entitled "Great Thinkers of the Past," written by major historical figures. It was a joy to have an intimate understanding of their ideas. However, one wonders, what were the thoughts of the not-so-successful people of the writer's era? How about the person who cut Rousseau's hair; or the poor devil who cleaned up the droppings from Hannibal's elephants?

Most of us assume that our ancestors were all great people. I remember my grandmother describing her father, my great-grandfather, as a "railroad man." She gave the impression that he ranked right up there with Leland Stanford. When my grandmother passed away, I found a photograph of my great-grandfather looking very distinguished, holding a stop sign at a railroad crossing.

If all the stories about ancestors being among the first settlers in the Plymouth Colony were true, there must have been 2 million of them standing on the rock at the same time.

Now at the time Newton was considering gravity, Copernicus the planets, Plato the Republic and Shakespeare the sonnets, what do you suppose my ancestor "Malaprop" Forman was thinking about? Why didn't he write an essay on his thoughts while chopping wood? It's reasonable to assume that Malaprop had no idea what an essay was and, even more importantly, that no one would have cared what he thought. Yet had they asked him, he might have had something to say.

The noted philosopher Michel de Montaigne devoted part of an essay to discussing what could best could be described as part of his private parts. He felt that it had a mind of its own, choosing to exert itself when its master wished it wouldn't and equally unwilling to perform when its owner would have deemed it highly desirable. I am certain that Malaprop pondered the same phenomena and might actually have provided insights equally illuminating.

All of this is simply a preface to the idea that views ought to also have been expressed by those whom history would otherwise ignore. Perhaps Malaprop sat under a pear tree and was banged on the head with a pear instead of an apple. Might he have concluded, as Newton did, that something must have attracted the pear downward? Perhaps never having mentioned such thoughts to others precluded him from being among the historical greats.

There are millions of long-gone Malaprops. We can't, of course, ask them to write an essay or their memoirs, but that shouldn't deter us from asking one of their descendants.

In the absence of a clamor by others, I have asked myself to write about things that I think about. My focus is not as broad as the meaning of life or do dogs go to heaven; it simply reflects some thoughts on alumni relations, a field that I devoted 30 years attempting to understand.

It is my hope that in the chapters ahead we will explore the field of alumni relations in a personal way. We will look at self-image, history, design an alumni program, tell some anecdotes and not take ourselves too seriously.

Of course, I never really had a relative named Malaprop, but I did consider calling one of my dogs by that name. However, I did have ancestors by the name of Ettiene, who were French. There are members of my family who claim the name is related to French Royalty. My own research, albeit limited, established that one such named ancestor was found in a Dutch brothel and hung.

The previous paragraphs are evidence of why the working title of this book was once called "Ramblings." Its appropriateness will be even more self-evident as you read on.

—Robert Forman

THE UNIVERSITY

There are few earthly things more beautiful than a
University. It is a place where those who hate ignorance
may strive to know, where those who perceive truth who hate
ignorance may strive to know, where those who perceive truth
may strive to make others see, where seekers and learners
alike, banded together in the search for knowledge, will honor
thought in all its finer ways, will welcome thinkers in distress or
exile, will uphold ever the dignity of thought and learning, and
will exact standards in those things.

They give to the young in those impressionable years, the
bond of a lofty purpose shared, of a great corporate life
whose links will not be loosed until they die. They give young
people that close companionship for which youth longs, and
that chance of the endless discussion of themes which are
endless-without which youth would seem a waste of time.

There are few earthly things more splendid than a
University. In these days of broken frontiers and collapsing
values, when the dams are down and the floods are
making misery, when every future looks somewhat grim and
every ancient foothold has become something of a
quagmire, wherever a University stands, it stands, it stands and
shines; wherever it exists, the free minds of men, urged on to
full and fair inquiry may still bring wisdom into human affairs.

John Masefield,
Poet Laureate, England
1930-67

> ## SOCRATES ONCE SAID,
> "IT IS ILL-ADVISED TO
> ASSUME THAT OTHERS WILL CARE
> WHAT YOU THINK; THUS IT IS THE
> WISE MAN WHO SIMPLY TELLS
> THEM WHAT THEY ALREADY
> KNOW, ASSURING THEIR
> COMPLETE AGREEMENT."

WHO AND WHY

After all that talk about essays, the more erudite among you will realize that this book is not really using the essay form. I am not sure what an essay is. However, my association with hundreds of alumni directors over the years assures me that there are only two of them who actually understand the essay format and they are too smart to have bought this book.

We must blame Latin for not having words that describe former college students without reference to a neutral gender. Alumni are male plural, alumnae female plural. If you're from the East, they are both pronounced the same way. Alumna is female singular and alumnus the male counterpart, with nary a word that describes both sexes together.

To rectify this, people have invented new words such as alum and alums. My old high school Latin teacher, Miss Wood, would not approve. Thus, I will alienate the female readers by using the male singular and plural (the unfortunate common practice) and risk their deserved wrath.

People who choose to be alumni directors are, in the main, those who wish to move to higher-paid jobs in other university positions. Usually that means university fund-raising. Thus after two years in alumni relations, one goes directly to higher-paying jobs with titles that would make any banker proud. After all, when a major donor is called upon to give to Old Siwash, he or she expects to be courted by someone with an appropriate title. No one in educational fund-raising is less than a director, vice president or tsar. In fairness, many alumni directors are now called presidents. I will use the term director because I was never made a president and I am still pouting over it.

Why would one choose the field of alumni relations as one's life's work? EDUCATION! There it is in capitals with an exclamation point. You choose this field because you believe that education is the most important thing in life, with the exception of God, family and the football team. You fervently believe that education moves all things important: world peace, security, saving the environment, health, and all those things that politicians talk about and do little or nothing to resolve.

If you don't believe in the value of education, find another field, perhaps the aforementioned politics. Furthermore, you must believe that education is not the singular domain of college presidents, deans and faculties, but also that of former students, the ones who went through the system and are testing it in the marketplace and in the quality of their life. They have something important and pertinent to say about the process.

Alumni financial support is essential but so are their ideas, creativity and leadership. If millions of Americans are illiterate, unemployable, can't or won't read books, have no understanding of environmental concerns, have no appreciation for other cultures or beliefs, and still discriminate against those who don't look and act like them; need I say more about the need for education?

Alumni administrators are not able to wave a magic wand and make higher education responsible for correcting the ills of a nation or its people, but they certainly can enlist the nation's brightest and most gifted to help set the course. That is what being an alumni relations professional is all about and that is why one takes the lesser pay, the long hours and questions such as, "Is that a full-time job?"

Who are these alumni? Well, there are a lot of them. I would make up a figure, but there is always someone like Doug Dibbert, the University of North Carolina alumni president, who actually knows the number. There are millions, more than 280,000 at the University of Michigan alone.

They are the ex-students who never took an eight o'clock class, partied all weekend and waited for exam time to crack a book. They told their families that they studied 20 hours a day and desperately needed time in the sunshine during spring break.

Now don't get upset. I know there were those who studied, did their assignments on time, worked three part-time jobs and joined the Young Republicans. On campus, they were called nerds. Today they are the chairs of boards and the big men and women on campus are working for them.

During the early post-graduate years, their views of alumni associations are summed up in a few choice words: "They are always asking for money" or "I never hear from them except when they want something or are selling something." In addition, the university is often blamed for all of the individual's ills: "Never did get the job I wanted." "I married the wrong person." "No one told me that I shouldn't have been a lawyer and should have gone to a seminary."

Of course, these are not views shared by people like us. We feel that college days were the halcyon days of our lives; that our degree has provided all the worthwhile things in our lives; that we shouldn't fire the football coach (winning isn't everything); and that our contribution is in the mail. Most alumni are somewhere in the middle of these attitudes, waffling back and forth.

An alumni administrator attempts to find ways of reaching graduates regardless of where they stand; using various approaches are used, to do this. There is bribery: "You want to sit on the 50-yard line, give generously." There is nostalgia: "Old Siwash has fallen on hard times; and old University Hall, where you first met Harry or Sally, is falling down." There is memory lane: "We will name a brick after you or Sally or your dog Fido to immortalize that precious time."

Today many alumni directors are entrepreneurs. They sell watches, travel, insurance, phone systems, bank loans, tires, toilet seats, caskets and will take in laundry. I must quickly add, lest the cynical among you get annoyed, that in my retirement I have added to this plethora by hawking several of the above.

The best approach to being an alumni director is to stop reading this book; go to your office; look in the mirror; and repeat, "I believe that it is important that people have the opportunity to explore ideas, increase their understanding of the world in which they live, know their past, think independently; and that their ability to do so should not be limited by social and economic restraints." Now I know this is a long sentence and many alumni directors will not be able to commit it to memory, so paste it across the mirror. If you believe in the sentiment, if not the choice of words, you are on the way to becoming an effective alumni director.

An alumni director ought to have a self-image that starts by seeing oneself as an educator and a leader. Your classroom is limited only by your powers of creativity. Your educational mission is to create an environment that reminds others of the importance of learning and to elicit support for the concept and participation in the process. Alumni professionals should also see themselves as advocates or even statesmen. You believe in educational quality, access, diversity and the mission of your university to accomplish these aims. You not only believe these things, you lead people to the same conclusions.

Do not assume that such a posture will be accepted by a majority of alumni; and be aware that others in the university community might also frown upon such views. Some faculty and administrators believe that education is their exclusive province and that you should promote credit cards. You will find, however, that there are serious-minded alumni and educators who will applaud you and begin to understand that there is depth and meaning to being an alumni professional, maybe sufficient enough for you to consider alumni relations worthy of your life's work.

SOCRATES ONCE SAID,

"WHEN LOOKING AT ONE'S SELF, ONE SHOULD SEE PERFECTION. IF NO ONE ELSE SHARES THAT VIEW, IT IS JUST ONE MORE OF THEIR SHORTCOMINGS."

SELF-IMAGE

So if this is to be your life's work, how do you prepare to do it? There are two approaches. One is to seek no advice. Rely totally on your common sense, personal charisma and the fact that your mother is on the board of trustees. The second, admittedly more difficult, is to take stock of your talents and experience. If you find that, you lack specific skills, attributes and dedication and you don't wish to learn them, then do not try to be an alumni director. Try something where such requirements seem less important, like running for political office. If, however, you conclude that you have some basis for creativity and leadership, then seek to prepare yourself in a variety of ways.

Let's consider self-image. Not all of us look like Cary Grant or Hugh Grant, although many I've known look like Ulysses S. I tried to think of a female Grant and came up with Kathy Grant, then realized I'm probably the only one old enough to remember her. I'm not certain what an alumni director should look like and it would be entirely chauvinistic to suggest that it matters. In fact, to demonstrate that appearance is not in any way important, I offer myself as an example.

Thus, when I speak of image, I'm referring to words such as statesperson, educator, advocate and leader. Once you give up your self-image as huckster and attempt to see yourself in these other guises and remain consistent, others will begin to appreciate these previously unseen virtues in you. They may no longer buy a used car from you; but they just might help you raise your particular banner in support of Old Siwash.

A lament often heard among alumni directors is that "I don't sit at the seat of power or counsel." This condition is not totally one's own fault. In some cases, those who preceded you have sat there until it was discovered they had nothing to say.

So before worrying about where you sit, think about what you might contribute if you did. Imagine a meeting with the president and executive officers, and you, the alumni director, are included in this august group. The topic is whether the tenure system is archaic and whether, instead of protecting academic freedom, it has become a means to maintain the "old boys" network and to discriminate against women and minorities. As each person comments, it becomes your turn. You look properly pensive and then say, "The association sold one hundred and twenty-two watches last year."

Your self-image should start by correctly assuming that you are a shaper and leader of alumni thought and opinion. You sit in such councils as a representative of one of the most important and powerful university constituencies. You, of course, don't speak for all alumni, but you are prepared to voice a considered opinion on their behalf. More importantly, you have created a cadre of alumni leaders perfectly capable of providing their own input, individually or through your representation.

In such councils, you can be, and indeed should be, the one person who is intimately familiar with the history and traditions of the institution. All alumni directors should be capable of giving a course on their university's history. Two of my predecessors at the University of Michigan wrote major histories and presidential biographies. Most university senior administrators' tenure is of short duration. Alumni directors can provide a badly needed sense of the past and a reminder of why things are as they are. On the outside wall of the Clement's Library at Michigan, there is a quotation that reads: "A people dwell in darkness that know their annals not."

Alumni directors can light the darkness. Armed with a sense of history, steeped in tradition and informed about matters of urgency on the campus, alumni directors can lead and be respected for their opinions.

SOCRATES ONCE SAID,
"LEADERS SHOULD ALWAYS LOOK FORWARD; THE SLIGHTEST BACKWARD GLANCE MIGHT FIND THAT NO ONE IS FOLLOWING."

LEADERSHIP

In every walk of life, there are people who make a difference. Some are affluent and powerful, others may be meek and humble. The qualities that suggest that they are leaders do not seem dependent on economic status or aggressiveness. To me, there are two prime aspects of leadership: creative ideas and the ability to articulate them.

As I view my own university experience, it seems apparent that the major contributions that have played a key role, both within the university and the alumni association, have emerged from the ideas of a few and not as a response from a groundswell of the many.

The initial concept of a university in Michigan was formulated before Michigan was a state. A territorial governor, a Catholic priest and a Protestant minister jointly conceived the idea that the then territory needed a public higher education program that would act as a capstone for the various schools and academies in the territory. It was a grand scheme, perhaps too ambitious for the time. However, when Michigan became a state, the seed had been planted for a state university.

Would there have been a university without the early ideas, respectively of Augusta Woodward, Gabriel Richard and John Montieth? Most certainly. Would it have been viewed as a capstone of a statewide educational system? Perhaps not. Others may have seen the virtues of a higher educational institution, but it took three dedicated individuals to start the process and set the goals.

The first president of the University of Michigan, Henry Phillip Tappan, came to Ann Arbor with his own concept of what a university might and should be. He wasn't hired by the regents to reflect the views of an informed and dedicated public. He was hired because he had ideas as to the nature of a quality university patterned after his own experience in Europe. A board of regents that could not match his creativity and ingenuity later fired him. The university was too young to have enlightened alumni leaders who might have stood up for him.

In the early 1960s, a handful of board members of Michigan's independent alumni association decided that alumni might enjoy a family camp experience. They were not responding to letters and queries from the alumni body but reacting to their own interest in camping, stemming from Boy Scout and similar experiences. Their ideas were not staff-driven or university-directed. They succeeded; however, in having the association buy a private children's camp on Walloon Lake, Michigan, consisting of nearly 400 acres, with a mile and a quarter of waterfront, and 52 buildings, The purchase price was $230,000, which the association did not have. The small group of alumni leaders, aided by a supportive staff, sold "camp bonds" at five percent interest to raise a down payment and took a 15-year land contract for the remainder.

Today more than 100,000 alumni and their families have enjoyed recreational, educational and social experiences in a magnificent setting. Third-generation pioneer campers are participating. The value of the site and facilities has appreciated to millions of dollars. Would it have happened without leaders with creative ideas and the ability to articulate them? In this case, I would have to say no.

Almost every major step in building a viable alumni program at Michigan has come from a limited group of leaders who would not have described themselves as leaders but as people with commitment and interest.

A partial list of their accomplishments includes the initial establishment of a self-governed alumni association, the first annual fund, the establishment of the first alumni university in America, the creation of a women's internship program, the concept of a center for the continuing education for women, the recruitment of underrepresented minorities, the initiation of educational travel, life-long learning programs on campus and the establishment of constituent societies in each school and college as well as constituent groups within the association for minority alumni.

Each of these events was initiated, in the main, by a few alumni and staff who seized upon ideas and made them work. One might draw the same conclusion about all aspects of life. In each community, there are people who make a difference. You see them in the local United Fund, churches, community agencies, school boards, special interest groups and political parties. Are they responding to needs, charting new courses and even satisfying their own egos? The answer is yes. In fact, the ego question is worth noting. My own view is that people with strong egos and a high degree of pride make excellent leaders. They fail miserably, however, if their ego is not matched with a similar degree of creativity and imagination.

The point is that if you develop an alumni relations program where numbers are the means of identifying success—whether the number of computer queries, members, gifts, sales of merchandise and or other such indices—you may find a large, financially viable and even acclaimed association that unfortunately can number its major contributions to education on one hand.

T. Hawley Tapping, a predecessor of mine at Michigan in the days of limited budgets, would travel westward from Ann Arbor on a transcontinental train, visiting alumni clubs scattered across America. As the train stopped in various cities, he would hop off and, with prepared lists of names and some nickels, he would call local alumni leaders and say hello. In the short duration of a train stop, he might only call two or three people, but each recipient felt important. Tapping knew who the leaders were and how important it was to cultivate them.

Here are some only slightly tongue-in-cheek methods of attempting to determine who among the alumni body might be a potential leader. Do they know the words of the alma mater? Do they get a tear in their eye when singing it? As undergraduates, were they involved in activities such as community service, homecoming, and student organizations; and did they attend sports events? Did they take advantage of the arts and cultural programs while on campus? Did they receive a scholarship or financial aid? Did they support their college experience by working part-time?

SOCRATES ONCE SAID,

"THE ACADEMY IS A PLACE WHERE THE SAME QUESTIONS ARE ALWAYS ASKED, ONLY THE ANSWERS CHANGE."

OLD SIWASH

Why don't we, for the fun of it, build a new alumni association for Old Siwash? We will use your ideas and mine and we will argue about those things on which we disagree. We will resolve any differences in the traditional academic way, with plenty of open debate, a thorough dialog on the issues, and an examination of the research, and then we will let the president decide.

Old Siwash has 125,000 living alumni and, believe it or not, we know where 80 percent of them are living. Few people have had the opportunity that we have to design an alumni organization from the start. The one assumption that we will make is that the alumni body is not that of a new university but is representative of a hundred-year-old institution. Thus, we must be concerned about alumni of all ages and economic diversity. As to ethnic, racial, religious and social diversity, we will make the assumption that diversity exists but is not necessarily representative of the population in general. We will assume our university is state-assisted but also dependent on major private support to function.

Old Siwash is blessed with a computerized address system complete with most e-mail addresses and has a modest amount of biographical data. If these had not been in place, they would have been a basic requirement that would precede all other organizational requirements.

Before we consider our first organizational steps, let us think a bit philosophically. What is the purpose or mission of our fledgling association? Can we define a simply stated set of objectives?

Now most "How To" books have numbers associated with them: five ways to lose weight, three easy steps to wealth and happiness, learn German in six lessons, or for that matter, the Ten Commandments. Just like the "How To" books, let us pick a number that will facilitate our tasks.

I say four premises. You say seven. Why? You like the number seven. Okay seven, but you will have to add the additional three. My first two premises are:

1. To support and sustain Old Siwash by organizing the alumni body as active participants in the university community.
2. To provide services and programs to the alumni constituency to enhance their life-long learning and to continue the bonding between alumni and alma mater.

Your turn:

3. To provide opportunities for alumni to play a dominant role in the governance of their own association to assure input that represents their attitudes and views.
4. To create an organization that recognizes that alumni, as former students, have special insights into the quality of the educational process and are testing that process in the marketplace and in the quality of their lives.

Aren't your two just like my first premise?

You agree, but you think yours are better stated.

The next one is mine:

5. To develop program priorities that reflect the needs of all members of the public, assure access for all qualified people and promote diversity for the betterment of all members of the university community.

You say my suggestions are too long-winded.

Okay, we will edit for brevity later.

Your turn:

6. To create opportunities for alumni to be involved in their individual schools and colleges and to participate in committees that normally have representation from students, faculty and administrators.

Don't criticize me for long-windedness.

Now my turn:

7. To create an organizational approach that encourages financial support from the alumni constituency in the form of memberships, to allow for greater financial independence and a sense of ownership.

You disagree with number seven because you believe it conflicts with alumni giving and causes confusion in the alumni body? I will delete it if you can show me just one study that actually proves your point. It is one of the myths of alumni fund-raising. In truth, there is ample documentation that dues-paying members of alumni associations provide a substantial majority of the private donor base. Members do not replace donors; they enhance the donor numbers. Most enlightened development officers encourage active alumni membership programs.

Note that we haven't specifically dealt with the question of independent (self-governed) versus dependent alumni associations. I prefer the concept of a self-governing organization of alumni coming together to serve their alma mater and themselves; but in reality, the president of Old Siwash is insecure and does not want an independent alumni association. It could be a threat to her leadership and sense of security; so what we will settle for is the idea that, although the organization resides inside the university's organizational structure, its policies and leadership selection are in the hands of an elected alumni board.

The president may not like this, but she still has institutional control. In addition, we were clever enough to put Old Siwash's former board of trustees' chair and major donor on our founding committee, creating clout of our own.

We now have some founding principles, albeit crude and not too well crafted. Nevertheless, it gives us a start and we will modify them as we move along.

Now the tough part: what should the organization look like? Let us start with a basic infrastructure upon which we will eventually superimpose other entities. We have a records program so we don't need to invent that. I would suggest that we examine a traditional infrastructure to see if it might still serve many of our needs.

Traditional organizations would include clubs, reunions, constituents groups (schools and colleges), special interest groups and print media (magazines, periodicals). In the traditional programs, we would create educational programs, campus reunions, educational travel, scholarships, financial aid assistance, student recruitment, placement services, donor cultivation, public support and actual fund-raising.

Today we are blessed with the capability and the capacity to communicate electronically with alumni in near real time. We can provide timely information, access to university resources and services. We can create an electronic environment that presumes that the student turned alumna is never estranged from the university.

However, we should be careful not to let the wide scope of electronic communication compromise our need to have programs that stress personal relationships for leadership recognition and development. Remember our original premise that significant developments on campus and within alumni associations are often created by a small group of leaders. To put it another way, we still need opportunities to have hands-on experiences. The way we get such experiences is to establish, in our infrastructure, those elements that allow for personal contact and representation.

Thus local clubs and chapters, class reunions, constituent groups, alumni universities, etc., all allow for the opportunity to meet and know alumni on a personal basis. In addition, such activities require volunteer leadership, thereby providing an early opportunity to evaluate potential and cultivate leadership.

Dr. Donald Morris, former president of Olivet College, in writing his doctoral dissertation, observed that prior to the University of Michigan's first major capital campaign, a major donor prospect list was prepared. At the end of the campaign, Morris was able to review the backgrounds of those who actually gave to the campaign versus those who did not. No alumni director would be surprised to learn that the major differential between the donors and non-donors was that the donors had a long-time relationship with the activities of the alumni association.

However, the activities associated with the more traditional alumni programs, almost by definition, are activities that attract a decided minority of alumni. A typical alumni club meeting may well have less than five percent of the available alumni in the area. This is not only a reflection of the amount of interest but of the competition for time availability. Yet those who do attend clearly have a strong motivation to continue a relationship with their alma mater. Any alumni professional worthy of the title can quickly assess leadership qualities among those who participate in such functions.

The Council of Alumni Association Executives (CAAE) is an organization of individual alumni directors from associations that are among the largest in the country. Their surveys indicate that between 20 to 30 percent of their collective alumni bodies contribute annually to the university. Similarly, about the same percentages are members of dues-paying alumni associations. Clearly there are far more non-donors and non-members than those that participate. Yet any Fortune 500 company would be pleased to have a 30 percent penetration of their available market.

The distinction that needs to be made is between broad-based communication and personal cultivation. They both have their place. People who have frequent electronic contact with their alumni association/university have a sense that they are still are a vital part of the university community.

It enhances the concept that the relationship between a student and the university is indeed life-long.

Steve Grafton, current president of the Alumni Association of the University of Michigan, has been a leader in developing electronic communication with alumni. I find that as an alumnus and user of this service, I have a continual and important relationship with the university. Grafton also has championed programs that relate to alumni on the basis of age, crafting specific opportunities that coincide with the current stage in one's life cycle.

The question that remains for all relationships with alumni is perhaps best described by an alleged incident involving the late Winston Churchill. Churchill was in the British Parliament when it was announced that an undersea cable had been successfully laid between Britain and the African continent. The parliament was in an uproar, cheering the news. When the noise subsided, Churchill rose and queried, "Now that you can speak to Africa, what is it that you wish to say?"

Now that we can speak to alumni, what is it we wish to convey? Historically, alumni directors were hired because of their editorial skills. They were chroniclers of university happenings, astute observers of the campus scene and editorialized on any matter they deemed important to alumni interest. They were the alumni "eyes" on campus.

They also were purveyors of alumni news, often on a personal basis. Who married whom, who got a new job, birth announcements, promotions, etc. In fact, for years the most-often read pages of alumni magazines were the class notes and the necrology sections. In the latter case, it was important to know who passed away. In the former, it was equally important to be able to measure one's own life by the success of one's classmates. The same information is still of prime interest to alumni today.

I used to have an alumnus from New York City who would call me once a month. The alumnus would always start his conversation with the lament, "The New York papers never have anything about Michigan." From there we would roam through news about athletic teams, student behavior, questions about his old school (Business Administration) and whatever else was on his mind.

Is every alumnus that interested? Probably not. However, any news article or report that starts with the mention of Old Siwash immediately gets one's attention. While in Florida in the winter, I frequently have been disappointed when seeing a news headline about the U of M only to find they were referring to Miami, not Michigan. Thus when we think of what to communicate, we need not engage in readership research. Just picture yourself a hundred miles from campus and think about the information you are beginning to miss.

Alumni directors need to write and communicate their own views. Editorials, essays, opinions of any sort are fair game. After all, you are the alumni agent on campus. Tell them what you observe and what you think about it. Whether your readers or viewers agree, you will make them think about matters of importance.

Are there limitations on conveying your personal opinion? In my judgment, only two: be constructive and don't deal in personalities. At one time or the other at Michigan, I risked the wrath, and on occasion gained it, of presidents, regents, deans and student leaders. In no case was it enduring; and, in most instances, their responses gave me a publishable reply and further insight into a concern.

University community members need to view the alumni voice as important, informative and worthy of attention. University administrators need to view alumni directors as important conveyors of alumni viewpoints and university information to alumni. If old blabbermouth is going to talk to all those potential donors, it's best that he or she knows what's going on. Thus, access to the "table" would seem essential; and again, once at the table, one might actually have something to say.

As I write this book, it occasionally dawns on me that someone like my old colleague and friend Dan Heinlen, former president of The Ohio State University Alumni Association, might be reading it. Heinlen would be disappointed that I haven't insulted him yet. Thus in order to simplify things so that he might better understand, let us summarize a few important points to date. (Also, it gives me a chance to fatten up the book, since I can see that I'm running out of ideas.) Heinlen, if given the opportunity, would quickly suggest that I ran out of ideas on page one.

Important thoughts:

- ▣ Create a self-image and hold fast even if others don't immediately accept it.
- ▣ Earn your way to the table by making others see that you belong there.
- ▣ Know your institutional history.
- ▣ Express your opinions and insights.
- ▣ See yourself as the alumni person on campus.

You are an educator and a statesman, not a huckster. If unable to do the above, marry the son or daughter of a major donor.

So, have we designed an alumni organization for Old Siwash? Well, actually not, but we have developed an infrastructure upon which someone as gifted and as bright as you can overlay a program designed to meet the unique needs of your university.

SOCRATES ONCE SAID,

"AS WE GROW OLDER, ALL OF OUR LIES BECOME TRUTHS."

ANECDOTES

Thank goodness for spell-check. I never could spell anecdotes. Remember somewhere back when you were fighting sleep, I suggested that alumni work was fun? Well it's not only fun but also rewarding in a very personal way. Let me share some experiences, all of which have little to do with the university, or at least not in a profound way.

You'll recall that I said significant ideas often come from small numbers of people and are a product of their creativity and not necessarily the result of popular demand. I wrote about the creation of a family camp at the University of Michigan that, not surprisingly, is called Michigania. It is operating in its fifth decade and is now a year-around program. Spinning off from this very successful alumni-created activity have been several other camps in other geographical areas. One of them was in Switzerland in the town of Montana. This Swiss program ran for 25 years and I had the pleasure of directing it. (I know you're thinking it was a tremendous sacrifice on my part, but someone had to do it.)

In the early days of the Swiss program, our attendees numbered well over one hundred. Later the numbers were smaller due to rising costs and the devaluation of the dollar. Montana is a French-speaking town located in the high mountain country of the Swiss Canton of the Valais, some 5,000 feet up a mountainside in a resort village famed for its winter skiing and summer spa activities. The town overlooks the Rhone Valley.

The alumni association leased a very successful international children's camp, La Moubra Sports Center. Run by the family Studer, it was and is the perfect site for such a program. At the camp, we offered faculty seminars, hiking, tennis, swimming, mini-golf, horseback riding, and explorations of the area by foot, van and bus. We visited Zermatt, the Matterhorn, Berne, Grindlewald, Lucerne and small mountain villages.

For whatever reasons, the environment simply brought out the best in all of us. Several weeks before the start of our first program, I received a call from an alumnus, who I knew personally, telling me the sad news that his wife had unexpectedly passed away. They had a young daughter, age 12, and he had concluded that he should cancel his trip. I suggested that he might wish to wait and see if the experience could be of some help in his daughter's obvious difficulty in adjusting to her profound loss.

They did elect to travel to Switzerland along with 180 others, including 80 under the age of 18. At our first orientation, I was presenting an overview of our program, going through our day-by-day itinerary. I mentioned our visit to Berne. I asked the group a few questions about the Swiss capital and was surprised when the little girl's hand shot up in response to nearly every question.

I complimented her on her knowledge of Swiss government and she responded that her teacher had taken some personal time to tell her about Switzerland. A gifted teacher, obviously cognizant of the child's tragic loss, had helped take her mind off her mother's passing by helping the child prepare for her trip to Switzerland.

The next step was easy. I simply called upon her each time we discussed some aspect of Swiss culture or history. The group began to call her "our little professor" and both she and her father were greatly comforted by the experience. It is the kind of experience that is not identified by statistics or fund-raising but is a major aspect of good alumni relations.

To add another dimension to this particular anecdote, we had on the same program, an elderly gentleman traveling by himself. He was a bit of a recluse and did not engage in any of the camp experiences beyond the seminars and excursions.

One evening we gathered on the side of the mountain around a blazing fire. We sang Michigan songs and camp songs from our collective pasts. The young girl was seated between her father and me and her lovely voice was almost strong enough to drown out my monotone, off-key sounds.

As we sang, I noticed the older gentleman standing above us on the balcony of our housing facility. I could see that he was moving his lips, singing along with us. I suggested to the little girl that she might walk up to the balcony and ask him to join us. You could see him bending over to talk to the child and subsequently she reappeared walking with the man clasping his hand.

He sat down by the fire and sang along with us. Later, the girl was sitting on his lap and as we closed the evening by singing our alma mater and America the Beautiful, there was a tear in many an eye. It was a special moment for each of us.

Alumni work is a series of little vignettes that create experiences difficult to quantify but that add a dimension to the work that cannot be reflected in compensation or other objective criteria. The camp experience in Switzerland is only a reflection of similar experiences with other programs. Club meetings, reunions, alumni universities, tours—all offer experiences that are difficult to measure but that have an effect beyond what one might expect and independent of the quantitative values of the activity.

Without embellishment, the following brief experiences speak for themselves. A woman returning for her 50th reunion has a wonderful time and writes us after her return home: "I enjoyed coming back to campus and seeing classmates that I haven't seen in fifty years. It served as a reminder of the wonderful times of my college days." Some weeks later, we received a notice from her lawyer that she was giving her home in La Jolla, California, to the Alumni Association upon her passing.

A 92-year-old man hiked in the Swiss Alps on our Swiss Alpine Adventure camp program. Upon his return, he attended the 75th anniversary of his high school graduation. There he met a woman that he had not seen during those intervening years. He asked her to marry him. She did and they lived together long enough for both of them to celebrate their 100th birthdays. He later told me that his Swiss experience was so exciting and reassuring that it gave him the courage to move on in his life and enjoy those remaining years.

Anyone who has escorted an alumni tour will tell you about the positive experiences that happen to many. I was fortunate to be in Meiringen, Switzerland, when an Ohio State alumni group was enjoying a program known as Alumni Campus Abroad. It was the last evening of their program and OSU Alumni Association President Dan Heinlein asked if any of the participants wished to say something. A woman stood and said, "As some of you are aware, my husband passed away this year and quite frankly I had no interest in making a trip like this. Fortunately for me, my friends encouraged me to do so. I can't tell you what a wonderful experience it has been. I have met so many new friends and I have so much more confidence in facing the future."

SOCRATES ONCE SAID, "THE THINGS WE SEE ARE NOT WHAT THEY ARE, BUT WHAT WE WISH THEM TO BE."

SOME PERSPECTIVE

In earlier days, the alumni director was often a close associate of the university president and was a one-person advancement officer. T. Hawley Tapping, general secretary of the Michigan alumni association for thirty-one years, was responsible for 12 issues of the Michigan Alumnus, four issues of a Michigan literary magazine, and 10 special football publications, in addition to his normal duties as alumni secretary. For years, he accomplished this output with a staff of no more than two.

The gift that these early leaders had was the ability to write and speak. They were hired for their communication skills, and they made good use of them.

The original organization of alumni general secretaries was formed in Columbus, Ohio, and was called the Association of Alumni Secretaries. Formed in 1913, it subsequently evolved into the American Alumni Council (AAC), which with the American College Public Relations Association (ACPRA) in turn became the Council for the Advancement and Support of Education (CASE). When the American Alumni Council ceased to exist, alumni professionals lost a major means of self-identification.

CASE used a new term, "advancement," and began combining several individual disciplines into a common family under the banner of institutional advancement. Of the various functional areas that were integrated under this concept, alumni administration was the only one that was not always a part of a university's advancement organization. Many alumni associations were governed by alumni, not by universities, and were designed to serve the needs of a university as well as the needs of alumni. As a result, not all alumni associations fit comfortably under the integrated advancement concept.

CASE has had difficulty determining a consistent course. The end result of a merger of the AAC and ACPRA, CASE struggled to be all things to all people. Its first president, Alice Beeman, was a gifted leader who saw correctly that her first mission was to heal the numerous rifts caused by the merger. She had to deal with malcontents such as Bob Forman of Michigan, who was a young rebel, chagrined that the new organization seemed to have abandoned the AAC objectives in favor of the broader scope of the entire advancement field. Beeman succeeded in bringing such people into the fold, ultimately encouraging them to actively participate in the new organization.

The merger caused the renaming and redistricting of old AAC and ACPRA boundaries and established an entirely new infrastructure. Beeman did her job well; and upon her retirement she left the new organization functioning with a solid staff and a group of volunteer leaders with a shared vision for CASE.

Jim Fisher, former president of Towson State University, was hired to succeed Beeman. (I must admit that my views of Fisher are influenced by the fact that I chaired the search committee that nominated him.) Soon after his hiring, I became CASE board chair. He became a close, personal friend and remains so today.

Fisher's vision for CASE was to establish organizational goals that provided for professional growth for individual CASE members and to enhance institutional appreciation and understanding of the role of the advancement field.

He was an eloquent spokesperson for the advancement field and was wise enough to establish within CASE parity among the various functional components. Thus, those of us in alumni administration felt that CASE saw our function as equal to other advancement elements. In addition, he had a special insight into the role of alumni executives, because he saw the similarity between his own job as an association president and that of the alumni director.

Fisher's own style could serve as a model for an association director. In the councils of Washington-based educational associations, his was a voice that was heard and respected. He was an author and a creative and philosophical thinker. Not everyone appreciated his style, perhaps in part because he saw the distinction between statesman and technician. That was an unsettling thought for those who did not aspire or qualify to be leaders.

Had health concerns not caused Fisher to retire early, CASE might have pursued its commitment to professional development to the profound advantage of individuals and institutions.

Fisher's successor was Gary Quayle. Quayle came to CASE with his own blueprint for its future. Perhaps he had been partially misled by the selection process. As a member of the search committee, I remember discussions suggesting that CASE needed a public relations effort to further establish its image both on campus and among those Washington-based educational associations.

Therefore, Quayle saw CASE as the advancement arm for education and the educational associations. He envisioned a Washington-based public relations program, administered by CASE on behalf of all education associations.

For various reasons, many CASE members did not accept this approach. Individual campus advancement officers saw the program as a threat to their own roles and others saw it as taking away from the need for CASE's commitment to professional development. The re-direction of CASE led, in part, to the dissatisfaction that prompted alumni directors to form CAAE, the Council of Alumni Association Executives.

It was during the Quayle administration that the parity between functional areas within CASE, so well established by Beeman and Fisher, began to falter. A senior vice president for educational fund-raising was appointed to supervise a vice president for alumni administration. Although announced as a temporary measure, it sent a message that alumni administration was, perhaps, no longer to be seen on a par with other advancement areas. It should be remembered that all of this took place in a relatively short period of time, from the days of the old American Alumni Council, wherein alumni professionals had their own national organization.

CAAE was founded, not just in response to the negativity described above, but more positively, due to the founders' desire to enhance the understanding of the role of alumni in university governance and counsel. The Council was in many ways the direct-line continuation of the objectives of the old American Alumni Council and the Big Ten Institute.

The Big Ten Institute was founded in the early 1970s. It was an idea that I introduced to my Big Ten colleagues at a meeting in New Orleans. I would take full credit for the concept except there are those still living who have excellent memories. The truth is that I had just returned from a meeting of the Big Ten Development Directors Institute on Mackinac Island, Michigan. My view was simply: if they can do it, why not the alumni directors?

The Big Ten invited 10 other alumni directors from major institutions across the country. It was important to have directors that shared the concept of alumni self-governance and that faced many of the same management challenges as the Big Ten.

The Institute succeeded exceedingly well and the invitation list grew each year. It was at Big Ten Institute meetings that the CAAE concept was first discussed. I was privileged to chair a committee that met to design the concept.

It should be emphasized that CAAE initially attempted to be a part of CASE, on some mutually agreed upon basis. OSU's Dan Heinlen and I met with Gary Quale and discussed CAAE's desire to do so. Quale reported that the CASE board felt it would establish a precedent for other organizations; in retrospect, not a very astute decision.

To the credit of the Big Ten, they unanimously voted to dissolve the Big Ten Institute and grandfather its participants into the newly conceived CAAE. Thus, all Big Ten Institute members became founders of CAAE.

In founding CAAE, we were not clever enough to find an acronym that had a meaning. Although I did recommend that we call the fledgling organization the Council for Rational Alumni Professionals, my esteemed colleagues found for some reason that the acronym CRAP was unacceptable.

Early alumni associations were mostly self-governed or, as I prefer, independent. They were organizations of alumni that came together out of the individual graduate's desire to serve the university and, for that matter, themselves. They were initially funded by subscriptions to alumni magazines and later by membership dues. In fact, in 1964 when I joined the Michigan alumni association, members were still referred to as subscribers.

Today the vast majority of alumni organizations can be referred to as dependent entities. Dues may help fund them, but they are part of the universities' advancement organizations and their directors report to someone within the administration.

CAAE has approximately 80 members as of this writing. Sixteen or so are members of independent associations. It should be remembered that CAAE is not an organization of associations or institutions, but individuals. As previously stated, CAAE had grown out of the Big Ten Institute. The Big Ten itself was one of the remaining strongholds of independent alumni associations.

When CAAE was founded, it was agreed that it would attempt to sustain, if not strengthen, the concept of alumni self-governance. Since its members were individuals, they could advocate self-governance regardless of the actual nature of their own association.

It is folly to think that there will be any conversion from dependent to independent associations regardless of what names we choose to use. As mentioned before, many university administrators are anxious about alumni involvement in university governance. They want alumni resources but aren't as keen on their ideas – unless, of course, the amount given is substantial enough to warrant some degree of tolerance.

In addition, the need for private support for public and private institutions has led to the idea that the foremost objective of university advancement is the raising of funds. Many fund-raising consultants have the view that alumni relations needs to be a subordinate part of the university's development program. As a result of this environment, CAAE defined its membership as individuals, not associations, so that the members could at least preach the virtues of alumni self-governance without the burden of the reality facing most of them.

CAAE has adopted a creed that states the fundamental principles of the organization. I am proud to have authored its initial draft. The final approved version is as follows:

CAAE CREED

"The Council of Alumni Association Executives (CAAE) is an organization of individuals committed to providing opportunities for enhancing the role of former students in support of higher education. CAAE is composed of chief executive officers of alumni associations representing many of the nation's leading educational institutions. CAAE is committed to the recognition of alumni as a vital constituency within the university community.

The CAAE CREED is a statement of the collective beliefs of the individual members of CAAE. It represents their commitment to advancing higher education through alumni involvement and the professional development of CAAE members. The following articles are statements of these beliefs in summary form and are meant to present guidelines for the university community to better understand the diversity of opportunities for alumni service.

ARTICLE 1

Alumni have a lifelong commitment to their alma mater. Their capacity and ability to serve are limited only by opportunities for service made available to them. Their willingness to volunteer is limited only to the extent those opportunities are presented in ways that capture their interest and encourage their involvement.

ARTICLE 2

The campus community has traditionally emphasized the need for collective input from its varying constituencies for effective institutional governance. Such constituencies are often limited to students, faculty, staff and administration. CAAE believes that alumni should play an important role in providing input based on their views of the quality of their educational experience as demonstrated in their professional, vocational and personal lives.

ARTICLE 3

Alumni involvement is enhanced when alumni have opportunities to establish priorities and levels of service consistent with institutional values. Such service is accomplished best within an environment that appreciates that alumni self-expression and an independent voice are of great value to the educational enterprise.

ARTICLE 4

The recognized opportunities for alumni service include, but are not limited to, enhancing private and public support; recruiting students; identifying, communicating and advocating institutional needs to a greater public; helping in the design of educational products to meet societal needs, and assisting in developing a campus environment of quality, diversity and integrity.

ARTICLE 5

CAAE believes that alumni professionals are capable of providing a unique insight resulting from their participation both within the campus community and in their relationships with alumni in a broader external environment.

ARTICLE 6

CAAE believes that there is a variety of organizational frameworks for implementing an effective alumni relations program. However, it is important that, regardless of specific structure, provisions be made for opportunities for alumni to chart their own approaches for service consistent with institutional goals.

ARTICLE 7

Alumni opportunities for self-funding programs in support of institutional goals are predicated on a strong combination of volunteer and professional leadership. Such leadership is committed to income-producing programs that stand the tests of quality, integrity, service and, when appropriate, educational content. Entrepreneurial activities to support organizational funding, scholarships, faculty and student recognitions as well as programs of service and communication are to be encouraged as long as they meet the aforementioned criteria and are consistent with good business practice.

ARTICLE 8

CAAE believes that an alumni professional should be viewed as an educational statesperson capable of articulating institutional goals and needs. The alumni professional is frequently seen as the singular daily contact between the institution and a primary constituency. As such, the professional needs to be a two-way communicator, representing the interests of both alumni and their alma mater.

ARTICLE 9

CAAE believes that college and university presidents should value a strong, constructive and independent alumni voice and encourage the development of programs that enable alumni to be full partners within the university community. To further encourage such participation, alumni professionals should be given the opportunity to participate in senior level deliberations and thereby provide special insights into decision-making and governance.

ARTICLE 10

CAAE shares the common belief of the entire university community that higher education is fundamental to the quality of life for our society and its people. We believe that personal happiness, the prospect for resolving societal challenges, and a peaceful solution to the problems of peoples and nations is vested in the understanding that comes from education. Therefore, CAAE holds as its highest priority a commitment to maximize the opportunities for educated people (alumni) to assist in all ways possible the higher educational enterprise.

This creed was adopted unanimously at the annual meeting of the Council of Alumni Association Executives on July 29, 2003.

SOCRATES ONCE SAID,
"IT IS EASIER TO GOVERN
THAN TO LEAD."

SELF-GOVERNANCE

What is the argument for self-governance? It starts with one's concept of a university. If you believe that a university is a collegial community of students, faculty, staff and trustees, and that the university benefits by this collegial approach, then it should be a given that a part of that community should be former students. Alumni are the products of the educational system. No company builds products, places them in the marketplace and forgets about them. Redesign of any system calls for feedback; therefore, alumni input becomes essential to the quality of the educational process.

The advantage of the self-governed approach is that alumni feel that they are stockholders in their own enterprise. The alumni director works for the association and is governed by the association's own leadership policies. It is that independence that concerns some presidents and chancellors. However, it has been my observation that competent and confident presidents are comfortable with this arrangement as long as such associations are constructive in their approach.

In the right environment, institutional goals are arrived at through a collegial process that includes alumni participation. Presidents have long respected faculty governance groups, such as the faculty senate, and have a similar regard for student government organizations. The self-governed alumni constituency is no different.

As a self-governed entity, alumni associations have the opportunity to raise financial support for their own purposes and are largely limited by their own powers of creativity. Their entrepreneurial efforts can realize income for expanded programs of service to alma mater and fellow alumni.

If we concede that there is little chance that current dependent associations will become independent, then why bother with any effort to sell the virtues of self-governance? There are variations of these two themes that might allow for some movement toward self-governance. The obvious is to have an alumni board of directors to which the university administration might concede some power to develop policies, goals and programs within the confines of university-administered budgets and staffs. In fact, that is the case in many instances. CAAE members, in the main, represent such associations.

Given strong alumni boards with creative and articulate leadership, the university would be wise to vest these people with broad powers to develop alumni relations programs. Alumni would actually manage such programs in the interests of both the university and the alumni body. Such associations would nominate names for alumni representation on key university committees, assist in various search processes for key university hires, etc

During one presidential search at the University of Michigan, a former regent who was a past president of the alumni association chaired the alumni advisory committee to the board of regents. On the committee were two former presidents of other universities, one current university president, a vice president of another university, and leaders of industry and business. The committee was diverse with respect to minorities, geography and age. Clearly, the regents would have been hard-pressed to find a more qualified group of advisors.

Major donors are obviously important to any higher educational institution. They are sought after, cultivated and given deserved preferential treatment. Such people did not come upon their resources by winning a lottery. They are men and women whose success is dependent on their own acumen, leadership and wise counsel. If the university wishes to gain their financial support, it needs to realize that such people can see through the transparency of efforts that seek only their money and not their more personal leadership qualities.

Positions of leadership in alumni relations programs provide dual benefits to the university. By exposing potential donors to the needs of the university, they have a better understanding of institutional challenges and increased motivation to be of help. Even more importantly, such people have qualities that enable them to affect positive change in governance both at the university and within the alumni association.

The best investment that a university can make in enhancing its private support is to invest in the alumni relations program of its alumni association and to give it as much free rein as possible.

For reasons difficult to fathom, some fund-raising consultants continue to malign alumni associations, often calling for their subordination to university development offices. Such consultants either actually believe this or are of the opinion that development officers seek such arrangements. Since the development offices pay them, consultants are inclined to give them what they assume they want.

Development offices and alumni associations have common goals for university support, alumni service and cultivation. It is a mystery that in many instances competitiveness, if not outright hostility, exists. There is no need to subordinate one to the other, and leaders of both entities should have common access to the president and executive councils.

If there is any legitimacy in fund-raising consultants' concerns about an institution's alumni relations program, it stems from two sources: under funding and lack of representation at senior decision-making levels. Subordinating the alumni program to the development program rectifies neither of these concerns.

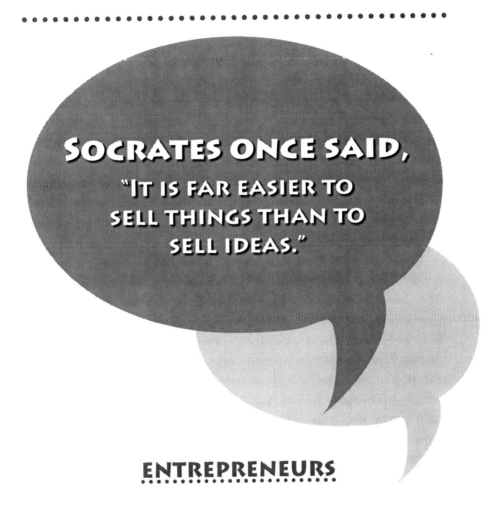

SOCRATES ONCE SAID,
"IT IS FAR EASIER TO
SELL THINGS THAN TO
SELL IDEAS."

ENTREPRENEURS

One current development in alumni relations might, unfortunately, lend itself to subordinated or merged alumni and development programs. That is the emphasis that many alumni directors have placed on income-producing activities. For years, alumni associations have added to their incomes by marketing certain programs that have provided services and income. Merchandise with university logos, travel programs and insurance products were some of the early promotions.

It was argued that university-related items in people's homes or on their wrists were simply good reminders of the affiliation with alma mater.

Tours with the accompaniment of faculty lecturers were seen as educational and the early insurance programs were largely term-life programs and served a niche in alumni careers.

However, the alumni marketplace experienced a major change with the introduction of credit card programs. Income realization far exceeded anything previously experienced. No one made the argument that such a program met a need or provided an otherwise unavailable service. Alumni directors, myself included, simply rationalized that someone was going to do it, so why not us. Furthermore, it was easy to argue that the income could be used for a plethora of good things such as scholarships, student aid, and faculty awards.

Credit cards then led to a bevy of other possibilities: phone programs, financial investments, car and homeowners insurance, to name a few. Universities also could see the benefit of such activities. Athletic departments, university hospitals, student organizations all jumped on the entrepreneurial bandwagon—or at least they wanted to. Such activities began to brand alumni directors as promoters, not leaders. More importantly, many alumni directors were gifted salespersons and succeeded in raising previously unfathomable income. University administrators could see the advantage of such marketing ventures to alumni, students and staff. The question, still unanswered, is where such activities might eventually reside.

Should alumni directors simply be turned loose to raise such funds with the benefit accruing to the university, or should such activities be vested in development offices or business offices? Perhaps universities will create new departments, perhaps an Office of Entrepreneurial Income.

If alumni directors emphasize their role as income producers, what happens to the more traditional roles? Equally important is the effect on relationships with alumni. One of the most frequent criticisms of alumni associations or universities is that "The only time I hear from them is when they want money." Will that be changed to "Whenever I hear from them, they are selling something?"

Yet with financially strapped alumni programs, can one really object to the desire to raise needed funds? Now add the issue of tax-exempt status. Non-profit organizations need to be mindful that their entrepreneurial activities should not put their exempt status in jeopardy. Many associations file their for-profit income as taxable, mindful to keep such activities at a level that does not jeopardize their non-profit status. Not being a tax lawyer or a CPA, I will leave this subject to others, except as a reminder that this is an area of concern.

SOCRATES ONCE SAID,

"TO PUT ONE'S REPUTATION AT RISK FOR A CAUSE DEEMED WORTHY IS THE SUPREME SACRIFICE."

COMMITMENT

Historically, some alumni directors have lived dangerously. One such person was Jack Fullen, former alumni director at The Ohio State University. In the early 1960s, Ohio State had won back-to-back Big Ten football titles, thus qualifying to go to the Rose Bowl in consecutive years. Fullen felt that this would be an overemphasis on football and would detract from the player's role as student. He led a faculty charge against Rose Bowl participation and succeeded.

It was my pleasure, as a new Big Ten director, to meet Fullen. He welcomed me at my first Big Ten directors' conference by asking if I knew who he was. I said that I did. He replied by wondering if it wasn't because of his difficulties with Coach Woody Hayes over the Rose Bowl question.

I answered in the affirmative. He reminded me that he had been hung in effigy on campus and had survived by the narrowest of alumni support. He went on to say that he was proud of the stand that he had taken and that there was too much emphasis on intercollegiate athletics. That was in the early Sixties. Imagine what Fullen would think today.

I always admired him for his stand, as I did when former Illinois Alumni Director Jim Vermette put his job in jeopardy by taking a similar stance against alleged wrongdoing in the Illinois athletic department. As I suggested before, alumni directors need to be constructive and not deal in personalities, but there are times when candor and honesty are necessary for the good of the university.

SOCRATES ONCE SAID,

"TO BEST CHART A COURSE FOR THE FUTURE, ONE SHOULD LOOK BACKWARD. ONE FINDS THE PATH WELL MARKED."

STANDING ON THE SHOULDERS OF OTHERS

I was most fortunate when I became an alumni director. To be candid, I could barely spell alumni let alone understand what the job was all about. I was fortunate for several reasons. I had colleagues within the alumni association who had been with the organization for years. They had worked under T. Hawley Tapping, a former president of the then American Alumni Council and the alumni director at Michigan for 31 years. In addition, my immediate predecessor, Robert O. Morgan, had been in that association for more than 30 years. He had a close personal relationship with longtime alumni leaders and was invaluable in introducing me to people who were important to the association.

These people were a font of information and I did not hesitate to seek their advice. I asked Morgan to stay on as an advisor and, aided by my other colleagues, I set out to learn on the job. Two others need to be identified by name: Harold Wilson and William Stegath. Both of these gentlemen had long associations with the alumni office and the university. Wilson had an encyclopedic knowledge of university history and a great sense of the importance of tradition. Stegath, a former Michigan sports announcer, was a constant reminder of the values of service to alumni as well as to the university.

Regardless of the amount of experience one has in the field of alumni relations, there is a need to understand the peculiar and specific history of a given association and university. I was blessed in having colleagues who understood this and were willing to "educate" me; but I had to ask.

In addition to the in-house counsel, I soon learned that my Big Ten alumni director colleagues were invaluable assets. The Big Ten directors met semi-annually. My first meeting was at Lake Delevan, Wisconsin; it was at this meeting that I met people who were to shape my professional career profoundly. I will list them, for each had a special gift that would be instrumental in my alumni education.

I mentioned previously Jack Fullen of Ohio State; although he might be described as irascible, he was a man of courage. He stood for principles that still need championing in higher education.

Loren Hickerson of Iowa often philosophized about the role of education in America and the part that former students play in assuring that universities meet the needs of all people.

Ed Haislett of Minnesota was a former college boxer; he was as pugnacious an alumni director as he had been in the ring. He was a pioneer in membership benefits, starting one of the early insurance programs as well as travel programs.

Joe Rudolph of Purdue is best described as a gentleman. He loved his alma mater and was a constant reminder of the importance of tradition. We learned not to snicker when he described Purdue homecoming events, including the annual march to the statue of John Purdue. For Rudolph, his work was a love affair and he instilled in me an appreciation of the emotions that alumni feel for alma mater.

Arlie Mucks was the alumni director from Wisconsin. His father had been a great Wisconsin athlete and an Olympian. Arlie was the personification of what others might think of as the sophomoric aspects of alumni, clad in red and white pants with Ws up and down the sides. He distributed Bucky Badger memorabilia everywhere he went. He had been a chamber of commerce professional and seemed to sell the university in the same manner that one might sell Wisconsin cheese. However, you soon recognized that this was a person who knew the importance of a public university and that he expected everyone else to share his enthusiasm and dedication. He was not selling cheese. He was selling a sense of pride in something he deemed profoundly important: education and the specific brand of education, which was the Wisconsin style.

Jack Kinney was my colleague from the state of Michigan. He was the alumni director at Michigan State University. Since my undergraduate education was at MSU, he was, in fact, my alumni director. Jack nearly got me fired in the first month of my employment at Michigan. Although I had a graduate degree from Michigan and had worked at the university for several years, there were many "Old Blues" that were content to reserve judgment about me. I had barely taken the position of director when, prior to a Michigan-Michigan State football game, I was called upon to speak at a joint UM-MSU pre-game "Crying Towel" meeting in Grand Rapids, Michigan.

Seated on opposite sections of the room were the grads of both schools. Michigan's attendees included some of university's most prestigious alumni, including Regent Paul Goebel who had been mayor of Grand Rapids, a great football player and Mr. Republican of Michigan. Goebel and I knew each other and I had reason to believe he had favored my hiring, yet I was very much intimidated by his presence. Others of near equal status sat next to him as I came over to say hello.

It was at this moment that my "friend" Kinney chose to send across the room a bevy of MSU cheerleaders to surround me and sing the MSU fight song. As I looked pathetically at the grim men of Michigan seated with their arms folded and looks of extreme displeasure, I realized that my future was hanging by a very thin thread.

Kinney was asked to speak first and gave a rousing pro-Spartan talk, pointing out how proud they were that one of them had been appointed alumni director at Michigan. I knew that my future was in the next few minutes. I couldn't be afraid to offend the Spartans. After all, Kinney had gotten me into this mess. I said that I was pleased to be there and that I had to candidly acknowledge going to Michigan State. I said that I appreciated the greeting by the cheerleaders, but that I hadn't recognized the song being sung. I said that when I was at MSU, the fight song was "Old MacDonald had a Farm." This, of course, brought boos from the Spartans and some cheers from the Wolverines.

I went on to say some insipid things, like although I enjoyed my days at MSU, I appreciated the opportunity to go to Michigan where I learned to read and write, wear shoes and eat with a fork. By now, the Old Blues were applauding heartily and the Old Greens were filling the room with catcalls. I followed these remarks with more serious comments about the tradition of the game, the great players who had played for both teams and the successes many of them had realized in their post-university careers. Needless to say, I was careful to use Regent Goebel as an example. I'm not particularly proud of my retort, but it might have saved my job.

Kinney was one of the few alumni directors who had the courage to move his alumni association from a dependent to an independent association. With the aid of enlightened volunteer leadership, he was able to establish a new and progressive association. Kinney, deservedly, was much admired by university administrators, including President John Hannah, an icon among the country's university presidents.

Unfortunately, one of Hannah's presidential successors couldn't fathom an independent alumni program. He virtually strangled the association by denying access to records, facilities and financial support. To Kinney's great credit, he fought valiantly to maintain an independent role for alumni. He used his editorial voice to keep alumni informed of the fight. He eventually lost both the alumni independence and his job. However, he demonstrated that alumni directors can be real leaders and can fight the good fight no matter how much the odds are stacked against them.

Kinney went on to great success as alumni director at the University of California, Santa Barbara, and remains one of the great elder statesmen of our profession.

Gene Vance was a former basketball star at the University of Illinois and a well-known and popular alumnus. Soon after our initial meeting, he became athletic director at Illinois. Vance understood the interdependence of alumni and athletic relations. I did not get the chance to know him as well as I did his immediate successor, Jim Vermette. I already have written of Vermette. He and Jack Kinney were cast in the same mold—articulate spokespersons for the right of alumni to be constructively involved in the governance of their universities.

Claude Rich was the alumni director at Indiana University. He and Jack Fullen were great friends and shared many similarities. Both were passionate supporters of the independent alumni association concept and zealous advocates for alumni participation in institutional governance. They loved their alma maters and were persons of considerable clout on their respective campuses.

The great benefit that I received from these past directors was their keen interest in the philosophical nature of the field of alumni relations. They were part of a generation of Americans whose careers started soon after the end of World War II. They were firm believers in the role education plays in the American Dream, that upward progression in attaining jobs and enjoying the quality of one's life are predicated on quality education. Many of them had attended college on the G.I. Bill. It was a serious matter for them and they felt their jobs played an important role in maintaining higher education objectives and making it available to all who qualified.

Often our alumni directors meetings went well into the night, with good-natured yet serious debate about the nature of alumni work. During the meetings, one had to be thick-skinned to withstand the barbs and comments of colleagues. If they felt you were exaggerating some aspect of your work or trying to impress them by stretching the truth, they would tell you so. These comments were often harsh and couched in words more often heard in bars than classrooms; yet, there was no lingering animosity between them. A heated discussion on one agenda item never carried over to the next.

In my initial meeting, I was to give a report on Michigan's fledgling travel program. In the middle of my presentation, OSU's Jack Fullen exclaimed, "You're nothing but a damn travel agent." Stunned and not really knowing what to say, I responded with the inane retort, "You're nothing but a Rotarian."

Fullen: "What the hell does that mean?"

Me: "Well, you have alumni clubs that meet on a regular basis, charge dues and have programs, just like service clubs. What is the purpose of those clubs?"

Fullen: "To talk about Ohio State, to keep them informed, to rally support."

Me: "That's exactly what happens on an alumni travel program."

Fullen was gracious enough to mumble something about, "You may do alright in this business." In retrospect, that may have been the nicest thing anyone ever said about my alumni career.

Those early meetings also had many humorous aspects, some of which I can't write about since I'm already in trouble over my reference in the Introduction to Michel de Montaigne's private-parts essay. Practical jokes were often outrageous—such as Fullen releasing the handbrake on Claude Rich's red Indiana staff car and pushing it into Lake Delevan, only to find the next morning that he had mistakenly pushed another red car, his own Ohio State vehicle.

Equally competent and dedicated persons succeeded each of these individuals and I was indeed privileged to learn from them. Frank Jones, who succeeded Rich at Indiana, was a person with a passion for history and a particular interest in Benjamin Franklin. He led a Big Ten commitment for recognizing the value of the Northwest Ordinance in shaping public education in America.

Ray Willemain became the alumni director at Northwestern. Willemain was a mentor and teacher to a generation of young professionals. He had an enormous effect on the profession of alumni relations. He became a national leader as chair of CASE and a highly sought-after speaker.

I purposely have not mentioned many of the current and recently retired alumni leaders. That's because there are many of them, not to mention that the process is certain to miss some and to offend others. Needless to say, there are similar "giants" today who are having the same effect on new people in the field that my early mentors had on me. In fact, I doubt there are any other professions where individuals are so willing to share ideas and experiences with each other.

SOCRATES ONCE SAID,

"A MISTAKE IS ONLY A MISTAKE WHEN WE FAIL TO ACKNOWLEDGE IT."

MISTAKES

Mistakes, I have made plenty of them. They are only mistakes if you do not learn from them. When I first became alumni director at Michigan, the association had not recruited new members for some time. This had a great deal to do with limited resources and other priorities. I came up with what I thought was a great idea—to give membership status to all donors to the university's annual fund. That is, if you gave a gift annually of equal to or more than the current annual membership dues, we would call you a member and extend such benefits. I know that it was a ridiculous idea, but remember, I was a novice.

Well, as you might expect, (inasmuch as Michigan alumni are not stupid) the current members, who also were donors, just dropped their dues and enjoyed membership benefits as a result of their gifts to the annual fund. It was the first of many such errors.

I corrected it quickly and began to pump scarce resources into membership promotions. I soon realized that the rate of return for each promotion covered the first year costs and if the member subsequently renewed, it was an excellent investment. Our renewal rates held to approximately 85 percent. Thus, membership promotion was then and is today the best possible resource investment.

Perhaps the most unsettling mistake I ever made resulted from a good idea. I much admired the work of Roy Vaughn, alumni director at the University of Texas. At a meeting of the then Big Ten Institute, Vaughn made a presentation on what I believe he called the upside down pyramid. His idea was that there was a point of contact within each alumni association between a staff member and the alumni constituency. Each point of contact was represented by an individual who was responsible for that area, for example, clubs, reunions, and travel. These were the people on the firing line, so to speak, and they were the important elements of the organization. The role of management was to support these folks so that they could do their job.

Thus, you would turn the pyramid upside down so that the large base was on top and the smaller management group was on the bottom—just the opposite of the normal organization chart. Now if Vaughn reads this, he will immediately lament that this isn't at all what he was talking about.

As my staff colleagues will tell you, they always were concerned about my return from a CASE, Big Ten or CAAE meeting, because I always stole good ideas and came back highly motivated to implement them.

In this case, I used Vaughn's idea and introduced to my colleagues my grand scheme for turning things upside down. I told each of the staff people who had direct responsibility for a program area that they were now on the top of the pyramid. They should look at their specific area of responsibility as if they were CEOs of a company. One company would run the alumni education program, another the travel program, another the family camp, etc. The role of the alumni director and the associate directors would be to provide the resources necessary to run these programs and to spend time creating new ideas and concepts.

The first group to become disenchanted was the former supervisors (associate directors) of major program areas, the people to whom the newly liberated "CEOs" had previously reported. They felt completely disenfranchised, lacked meaningful responsibility and missed the experience of actually managing people.

The newly assigned managers of their own enterprises had mixed reactions. Frankly, some of them who had always been able to blame any shortcomings on their supervisors now had to take personal responsibility. It was a new culture for them. Others didn't really believe what they had been told and still sought the approval of former bosses. Some indeed benefited by the change and set about pursuing their objectives "free at last."

In the main, things seemed not to have changed, except matters were more confusing. Finally we just eased back into the old ways of doing business with a slight increase in individual responsibility for program managers.

Was it a mistake? I can give you names of colleagues who will assure you it was. Was it my greatest mistake? I can give you the names of colleagues who will assure you that it was not.

SOCRATES ONCE SAID,
"WHAT WE SEEK WHEN WE ARE NOT WORKING SHOULD BE OUR LIFE'S WORK."

REFLECTIONS OF OUR OWN INTERESTS

No two alumni associations function alike and no two alumni directors function alike. We all use whatever strengths we have, delegate our weaknesses, and continually try to fit round pegs into square holes. The truth is that the magnitude of possibilities available to extend our outreach to alumni is virtually unlimited. The limitations are not always self-imposed but often products of limited resources and lack of the leadership vision of others.

It is equally true that since we can't do all things, we tend to do those that we have either a talent for or that give us some personal satisfaction. The result is that most alumni associations are the reflection of their director's ambitions, likes and dislikes. As a kid, I went to summer camp.

Later on, I worked at such camps. It is no mystery that the alumni family camp program at Michigan was strong.

Travel was always something I wanted to do and Michigan's travel program is a reflection of that. I grew up in a diverse blue-collar community witnessing the lack of advantages to people of working classes. The association's commitment to the recruitment of underrepresented minorities and the need for access is part of my own experience. I am certain that as alumni directors examine their own association programs, they will see that they reflect their own attitudes and desires.

This is the reason why many people leave the field of alumni relations. If your ambitions are not reflected in the opportunities you create, or that the association can afford, or in some instances, the university will permit, then you move on to something else. That is why educational fund-raising is often viewed as a natural move for alumni professionals. In most cases, it affords greater compensation, measurable accomplishment and a higher degree of order.

However, for those who stay in alumni relations, it offers a career worthy of one's life endeavor. To work on behalf of a university is a calling. Belief in the values of education provides an opportunity to feel that one can make a difference. In addition, you are working with volunteers and colleagues who share that commitment. In my more than 35 years at the University of Michigan, I had my share of down days and often self-made tribulations, but I never once doubted that I was fortunate to spend my working life in such a rewarding environment.

SOCRATES ONCE SAID,

"A WISE MAN LAUGHS LOUDEST AT HIMSELF AND LAUGHS WITH AND NOT AT OTHERS."

DON'T TAKE YOURSELF TOO SERIOUSLY

As I have mentioned, I learned a lot from my colleagues in this business. That is particularly true with my Big Ten and CAAE brethren. One gift they gave me is not to take oneself too seriously. Imagine giving a talk on professionalism to a Big Ten Institute session, and feeling good about the receptivity of your remarks, when it becomes readily apparent that no one is listening. You can see that their attention is focused on something occurring behind you. You turn to see Wisconsin's Arlie Mucks leading two dairy cows up to the conference room window, getting ready for the annual milking contest planned to occur during the coffee break—so much for a talk about professionalism.

The act of putting others down becomes a science in such groups. My favorite target was my friend Dan Heinlen. The Ohio State-Michigan rivalry was sufficient reason, but the fact that he was and is such a good friend makes it all permissible. Once when he was pontificating on some subject, I interrupted to suggest that in biblical times it was considered a miracle when an ass spoke. On another occasion when introducing him, I suggested that behind that smiling, affable face was a very shallow person. He, of course, was equally cruel and humorous with me, but I'm writing this book and therefore choose to include only my remarks.

Mucks was often the glue that kept our collective fellowship in such good spirits. As the perpetual conference administrator, he frequently was at a podium making announcements, etc. He would butcher people's names in his pronunciations, a little like Yogi Berra. I was never sure whether he was putting us on.

Our summer meetings of both the Big Ten Institute and CAAE were always in Wisconsin. There was nothing about Wisconsin that Arlie didn't love and promote. We ate cheese, brats and cranberries, wore red Wigwam-manufactured socks and had Bucky Badger signs on every inch of wall space.

Once in the long history of these conferences, Jack Kinney and I lobbied to move the summer meetings to Northern Michigan. Mucks pouted the entire conference. The only thing that cheered him up was the fact that it rained for three straight days and the group vowed to never return to Michigan.

Arlie instilled a spirit that might seem sophomoric to some, but it added immeasurably to the esprit and fellowship of the group and created an atmosphere of collegiality and sharing. Occasionally a pompous ass would show up among us and suggest that such antics were unprofessional and demeaning. Those types did not seem to fare well in alumni work. When you work seven days a week and several nights in addition, the need for a sense of humor and a chance to recreate is overwhelming.

The Arlie Mucks of our lives are badly needed. Don't for one moment think that he was not an excellent alumni director with every bit the professionalism of any other director. He also was a general in the Air National Guard and a statewide political figure.

Self-deprecating humor is also is a strength that alumni seem to appreciate. After all, when they attend alumni events, they want to learn, rekindle their collegiate days, but also have a good time. An able alumni administrator (how's that for alliteration?) should be able to deliver a meaningful message and at the same time make an event enjoyable. When you are looking out at a sea of unfamiliar faces, the best target for humor is yourself.

I liked to tell stories about some of the events that occurred while giving talks to alumni clubs.

My very first alumni club meeting was in the far reaches of Michigan's Upper Peninsula. Eagle Harbor is farther from Ann Arbor than Ann Arbor is from New York City. I had been invited to speak at a gathering of alumni from across Northern Michigan. For more than 700 miles, I practiced my speech, talking out loud as I was driving and ignoring the looks from passersby. I was well aware that many alumni still hadn't cottoned to the fact that a guy with a degree from Michigan State could be their alumni director. I decided that I would speak about university history, outlining the special accomplishments of each of the nine Michigan presidents.

I had already begun the process of learning as much as I could about Michigan history. Thus, as I arrived at the church in Eagle Harbor where I was to eat with the group and speak later, I was nervous but prepared.

When the moment came, the president of the local club greeted everyone, made a few announcements and then turned to me and said, "Our new alumni director, Bob Forman, is with us tonight. I am told that this is his first alumni club meeting since he was appointed. It would be a shame to make him earn his supper by giving a speech. Therefore, as we clean up the tables, my husband will take Bob, along with the garbage, to the bear pit (dump). Maybe they will see some bears. The rest of us will walk across the road to the shores of Lake Superior where we will build a campfire, sing Michigan songs and drink from the paper bags that I know you all brought along."

I have been told over the years that my non-speech was the finest I ever gave.

On my way back to Ann Arbor, I spoke to the Michigan Club of Cheboygan. There, I finally gave my speech. It seemed warmly, even enthusiastically received. Clearly I had demonstrated how much I knew about the university's history. The club president leaped to her feet and announced how thrilled she was to be reminded of Michigan's great tradition. She then turned to me and said, "For a perfect closing to our evening, I am sure that Mr. Forman would be pleased to lead us in the singing of our alma mater, The Yellow and Blue. It was then that I realized that not only did I not know all the words to the alma mater, neither did most of the audience. We hummed.

Jim Vermette, the former Illinois alumni director, tells the story of his first alumni meeting in Chicago. Like me, he was nervous and with the huge Chicago audience wanted to do a good job. As the evening progressed, there were a variety of introductions and short remarks leading up to Vermette's introduction as the main speaker. Just one more introduction was to be made, that of a former Illinois athletic great who not only stood but decided to give a short speech of his own. His recollections of Illinois' great athletic past brought the audience to its feet. In unison, they sang the Illinois fight song and the entire assemblage, filled with enthusiasm and good will, filed out of the auditorium, leaving poor Vermette alone at the head table.

Once at a meeting in Lancaster, Pennsylvania, I was introduced by the event chairman in the following manner, "I have heard Mr. Forman speak before." He offered no opinion to the quality of the talk, but as I approached the podium, he walked from the head table down the center aisle of the hall and out the door. Later I found out he was a doctor and had gotten a beep that called him to an emergency. Too bad the rest of the crowd didn't know it.

On another occasion, I had just started my presentation when a loud snoring erupted from somewhere in the room. Putting people to sleep was not a new experience for me, but to do so in the first two minutes was indeed a record. People in the audience began to look around to see who among them had nodded off. The snoring got louder, but there was no evident culprit in the room. Finally a fellow in the back row got up and walked around the partition that separated our room from the adjoining one. In the adjacent room, he found a fellow apparently sleeping off a cocktail party that had taken place earlier.

In a hotel meeting room in Wichita, Kansas, the hotel had set up a luxurious buffet, complete with a giant ice sculpture of a bull in the middle of the table. In the midst of my after-dinner speech, a man burst into the room in a large cowboy hat and a western shirt and tie. He obviously was inebriated. He shouted, "Has anyone seen my bull?" Spotting the sculpture, he ran to the table, lifted it to his chest and walked proudly out the door. It was some time before the audience was interested in what I had to say.

I wish I had known that when you have just introduced the new president of the university to a large alumni audience, you should not fall asleep during his or her speech;

1. If you do fall asleep, it really is bad form to let your head fall on the table with a resounding crash;
2. When introducing the president, it is important to use the name of the current president not the immediate past;
3. When returning with the president from the aforementioned meeting, it is wise while pontificating on everything you know to observe that the president has fallen asleep;
4. When attending a major fund-raising gathering hosted by the CEO of one of the country's largest beverage companies, it is wise, in his presence, not to tell the waiter that you would prefer the soda from his biggest rival;
5. When introducing the president of the United States to a gathering of hundreds of his fellow alumni, it is wise not to wear a light blue summer suit and run to the restroom minutes prior to the introduction.
6. If you do, don't compound the disaster by remaining in the men's room in front of the hand dryer, airing a strategic area until a colleague rushes in and shouts, "What the hell are you

doing? You are supposed to be introducing the president of the United States."

7. When you arrive on stage carrying a "protective" briefcase, don't be surprised that the Secret Service wishes to search it.

SOCRATES ONCE SAID,

"WITHOUT TRADITION, THE ECHOES OF THE PAST WOULD REVERBERATE IN A SOUNDLESS VOID; AND MAN WOULD THINK THAT HE WAS ALONE."

TRADITIONS

Each university has its own traditions. Obviously some have been in existence longer than others. At Michigan, I was blessed to be part of a university with a long and illustrious history. Its football team has won more games than any other university and has been in a neck-to-neck competition with Notre Dame for the best winning percentage. Michigan also has been blessed with a great musical history. Its fight song, The Victors, once was described by John Philip Sousa as the best in the nation. It has an additional fight song, Varsity, that is the fight song for hundreds of high schools in the country.

An all-male Union Opera also was the source of a litany of songs still sung by the men and women's glee clubs. Each of these songs has its own story and alumni are always delighted to hear them.

Charles Mills Gayley wrote the words to Michigan's alma mater, The Yellow and Blue. He had been born in China, the son of a missionary. His father died of cholera, leaving his widow and son to return to the United States. However, the Civil War prevented their return and they ended up in England.

After his mother remarried, Gayley was raised in England and admitted to Cambridge. However, an uncle in the United States urged the family to come to America and to enroll Gayley at the University of Michigan. He received three degrees at Michigan, later taught the antiquities and wrote a number of Michigan songs including the alma mater.

Another thing he taught Michigan students was a modified version of English Rugby football that evolved into the American version. According to some, this made Gayley Michigan's first football coach. Later, he wrote the alma mater for the University of California, Berkeley. His younger sister married a Michigan alumni director and was one of the founders of the Michigan League, a campus facility for women students.

I tell these stories because alumni find such recollections of great interest and it makes them proud of their tradition. Each university has similar stories with the same high degree of alumni interest. I find that often the alumni director is one of the few people on campus who has knowledge of tradition and history, due in part to the fact that the alumni director frequently has far greater tenure than the average administrator.

When the late Gerald Ford, a Michigan alumnus, ran for president, the Michigan fight song, The Victors, was played at his various fundraisers and speeches. I received some letters, mostly tongue in cheek, objecting to the use of the Michigan song. I would write back pointing out that the Democrats also had a campaign song dating to the Roosevelt days, Happy Days Are Here Again. That song is still played at Democratic functions. It was written by Michigan alumnus Jack Yellin.

There is a point to all these Michigan ramblings: know your history. Whatever the expertise of others in the councils of the university, you will have at least one area in which you are uniquely qualified.

SOCRATES ONCE SAID,

"To share what you think with others is a gift to be wrapped with reason and truth. To do less shames both the giver and the receiver."

OPINIONS

The alumni magazine affords excellent opportunities for alumni directors to make their views known. At Michigan, the alumni director also was listed as editor-in-chief of the Michigan Alumnus. At many alumni associations, the alumni director is listed as publisher. In these instances, there are opportunities to voice one's opinion in an editorial column or op-ed piece. Alumni magazines have a long shelf life and often are found on the coffee table. Chances are that your editorial eventually will be read, although most frequently after class notes and the necrology listing.

I often would get letters to the editor referencing an editorial written months prior. It affords the director the opportunity to address questions of concern and to generate an exchange of letters and opinions for future issues. Not so surprisingly, people on campus are quick to read such pieces, providing the opportunity to communicate with people with whom you might not normally have access.

By the way, I am aware of at least one alumni director who in the absence of an appropriate letter to the editor would simply write one himself. I won't name the director, but the letter writer was always called Dexter Thornapple.

There are moments on campus when a constructive and independent voice needs to be heard. That voice might be the alumni director, or the association chair, or president, or some other identifiable alumni leader. The alumni magazine, along with public hearings or meetings of trustees, provides opportunities to present views that represent an important university constituency.

Even in a totally dependent alumni association, the alumni volunteer board chair will be a person deserving of respect and attention by others in the university community. He or she can present views that cast light on subjects germane to alumni interest. At Michigan, such occasions were frequent.

During a time of attempted major cost reductions under the theme of "smaller but better," the administration attempted to reduce the scope or perhaps the very existence of several schools and colleges, and some special program areas. In an attempt to work their way through this exercise in a collegial way, they appointed review committees of faculty members from schools and colleges not being reviewed. In my judgment, this approach was a mistake. No one likes the thought that he or she may have to cut positions or do away with programs that represent his or her life's work; but such decisions are even more negatively received if the decisions are being made by faculty from other disciplines.

One of the units being scrutinized by this process was the School of Education. I wrote an op-ed piece for that school's magazine that went to alumni, faculty and students and, of course, the regents and administration. One of the criticisms of the school was that a large percentage of its graduates went on to jobs outside the state. I pointed out that if that were a negative, then we should abandon our famed Law School, where more than 50 percent of its graduates practiced elsewhere. I also observed that the School of Education had a far better record in attracting minority students and provided access for a more diverse student body.

As usual in such matters, educational quality was at issue. As is often the case, quality is a product of educational investment. The faculty of the school knew its own shortcomings and with the proper resources could have provided for whatever real or assumed qualitative deficiencies existed.

The real crux of the problem was that an institution that prided itself on the quality of its academic programs had made the unfortunate assumption that several of its colleges were the type that could be found elsewhere. It was an expression of academic elitism, in my judgment, encased in the guise of economics.

This attitude caused me to write an article for the Michigan Alumnus, which I entitled "Greatness for Whom?" The thrust of the article was that you can create a great university with the highest of academic standards, but if you don't make that quality education available to deserving students, what good is it? Underrepresented minorities were prevented from attending colleges not because of academic shortcomings but because of economic and social restrictions.

The Michigan alumni association helped pioneer the university's commitment to diversity and access. I am proud of the role that the staff played in developing programs and strategies; but the people who made a difference were members of the association's board of directors. Outstanding board leadership caused the association, as a matter of written policy, to declare that the recruitment of underrepresented minorities, students, faculty and administrators was to be the association's highest priority.

During the time the previously mentioned "Smaller but Better" theme was pervading the campus, I spoke at a public hearing concerning the School of Natural Resources. The obvious theme for that presentation focused on the worldwide need for environmental concern and the further need to have distinguished universities lead the way by maintaining quality programs and investing in their future as opposed to restraining or doing away with them.

When an institution drops, modifies or severely restrains schools and programs, it does an immense disservice to the graduates of those units. It says that the university does not feel that the program from which you received your degree is worthy of sustenance. An obligation of an alumni association is to protect its alumni from serious degree-depreciation. By the same token, there is an equal obligation to promote the growth in excellence of programs in order to provide for the enhancement and appreciation of one's degree.

The matters of concern to alumni seem endless, but without an organized alumni program, the voices of most will not be heard. Furthermore, if the only alumni voices to be encouraged are those of the most generous of donors, then the university will be influenced by a very limited base.

SOCRATES ONCE SAID,

"PEOPLE WHO WORK WITH THE HEART AND SOUL INSPIRE OTHERS. PEOPLE WHO WORK WITH THE MIND AND THE INTELLECT LEAD OTHERS. PEOPLE WHO DO BOTH ARE CALLED SAINTS."

ALUMNI LEADERSHIP

Volunteer leadership of an alumni organization is the reason for its existence. These are the people enfranchised by the association to speak for the alumni constituency. They come from all walks of life; and, if they are selected with some discernment, they should represent all the alumni constituencies including age, geography, schools and colleges as well as race, gender and other aspects of diversity.

Such a board may seem large and unwieldy. My own view is that they should be viewed as a faculty senate or assembly. They do not have to meet with great frequency, but when they do meet, they need to have enough time to properly deliberate and make sound decisions. The use of an executive committee can serve the need for more frequent meetings, but only under dire circumstances should such a committee act in the stead of the board.

It is reasonable to assume that graduates who have demonstrated success in every field of endeavor have ideas and advice worthy of the attention of all campus administrators and decision makers.

An alumni board that has bank presidents, astronauts, university presidents, judges, teachers, political leaders, professional athletes, doctors, movie stars and just good, dedicated, ordinary alumni, ought to be worthy of someone's attention.

I found that with such a board, I could just hang on and enjoy the ride, with an occasional gee and haw to sometimes change direction.

SOCRATES ONCE SAID,

"TODAY IS YESTERDAY'S
FUTURE. MAKE THE MOST OF
THE PRESENT AND
THE FUTURE WILL TAKE CARE
OF ITSELF."

THE FUTURE

It seems appropriate that we should spend some time thinking about the future. At a meeting of CAAE several years ago, several people were asked to comment on the future of alumni relations. I am afraid I was more negative than the others. My scenario emphasized the movement to more and more entrepreneurial activities. The success of such programs would lead universities to conclude that the opportunities for making money were immense and that the revenue should not be limited to alumni associations.

As a result, income from markets including alumni, students, faculty and staff would become an essential part of university funding. Separate offices would be set up to manage such programs and these functions would be outside the alumni organization. Thus, alumni directors might opt for positions within the new organizational structure or remain within associations with even more severe budget limitations.

Several indicators suggest that this view might be more accurate than I first imagined. Many new recruits to alumni work are assuming positions in marketing, membership or alumni benefits. With business administration degrees, they are hired because of their perceived business acumen and show little or no understanding of the objectives of an alumni relations program. Their purpose is to maximize earnings from programs that provide products and services to the alumni and student markets.

It is a flattering and ego-building process to be cultivated by large companies and corporations eagerly seeking your participation in a moneymaking activity. Seldom in business history do so many relatively young and inexperienced people have the opportunities to engage in moneymaking schemes of such magnitude.

In addition to the unusual opportunity this approach provides, many alumni directors seem content to allow these often-inexperienced people to operate quite independently.

In recent years, several geographically organized marketing groups have been created to bring people working in alumni marketing together. They have sought financial support for their various programs and activities from their business partners—on occasion, without the knowledge of directors and supervisors.

People who are negotiating and rewarding contracts ought to have knowledge of the objectives and purposes of sound alumni relations programs.

I recently attended a meeting of Canadian advancement officers under the aegis of the CCAE, the Canadian Council for the Advancement of Education. This conference was designed to bring together affinity partners and their counterparts within Canadian universities and alumni associations. The host university was the University of Toronto. That university has developed an excellent program by partnering with companies in a variety of businesses, including credit cards, insurance, travel, and merchandise.

The University's major affinity partners may support specific projects and are identified with those projects in university publications and promotions. The Toronto approach is to centralize all such activities under one office. The income derived from these relationships is held in a central fund and dispersed to support a variety of university-related needs. The alumni association is a player in this process. However, the income does not come to the association but to the centralized office.

Such an approach may well be the model for the future in the United States. Ironically, alumni associations' successes with affinity partners may lead to the demise of future income opportunities for the associations. If universities see the income potential developed by alumni associations, they will attempt to centralize such activities elsewhere.

University administrators may deem entrepreneurial income to have sufficient potential to establish such fund-raising activities on a par with gift income. Public universities could rationalize that tuition, state appropriations, private support, endowment income and entrepreneurial income would be a five-legged university support base.

Now that I have alienated all people under the age of 30 and have suggested a view of doom and gloom for alumni directors, let me back up and suggest what hopefully is obvious to all readers. There are alumni directors who have the talent and experience to perform extremely well in any environment, regardless of organizational design, independent or dependent or any variation thereof.

They will succeed in being involved in the senior ranks of university governance, manage to be major players in entrepreneurial and marketing activities, and play a significant role in the overall success of institutional mission.

These directors manage their income-producing activities and use these resources to meet association and university goals. They may employ entry-level people in marketing positions, but they manage such personnel by maintaining a relationship that will assure professional growth and responsibility. There are many such leaders in today's alumni profession and they have managed their programs by providing quality leadership through mentoring and education.

One should remember, however, that with more than 3,000 higher education institutions in the United States, most alumni organizations have only a few people to do a multitude of tasks. Even in the CAAE membership, there are gifted alumni directors, who are burdened by limited resources, attempting to match the accomplishments of their peers; and, executive officers who would prefer to invest in short-term fund-raising rather than long-term friend-raising.

The directors who have succeeded, regardless of the organizational situation they inherited, need to share their insights and experiences with their colleagues. Such sharing was one of the founding principles of both CAAE and CASE.

SOCRATES ONCE SAID,

"RELATIONSHIPS BEGIN WITH SEEING IN OTHERS THOSE QUALITIES THAT THEY WISHED THEY POSSESSED."

RELATIONSHIPS

There are several relationships within the university community that can be mutually beneficial; however, as obvious as this mutuality may seem, their implementation requires a positive effort on behalf of the alumni director.

University faculties often assume that the university exists only because of them. Students might argue that without them, universities would be empty hollow places. For our purposes, we will simply agree that both are essential to institutional existence.

An able alumni director needs to find ways to cultivate both entities. Faculties obviously have a high regard for students. If not, they should be in some other line of work. For some reason, once these same students become alumni, that regard seems to diminish. The suggestion that a former student might have some serious input into questions of academic substance borders on heresy for some academics. It ranks right up there with telling the football coach that he needs to pass deep more often.

The creation of school and college alumni societies (by whatever name), as well as the creation of alumni visiting committees, has somewhat allayed this attitude. Deans and faculties begin to see virtue in alumni input, independent of their asset as possible donors. At the University of Michigan, alumni of several schools have aided immeasurably in enhancing the quality and reputation of those schools with their ideas and counsel. In addition, from a development standpoint, the alumnus who feels that his or her ideas have value is more willing to respond to requests for financial support.

Involving faculty in alumni activities is an important means to developing mutual regard and understanding. The use of faculty as speakers at club meetings and alumni universities, and as tour escorts gives them an appreciation of alumni as life-long students, and dismisses the notion of more sophomoric qualities.

The establishment of faculty awards for outstanding teaching or the funding of faculty research projects are other ways to enhance the faculty-alumni relationship.

For alumni to see faculty members in non-traditional venues enhances alumni-faculty relations. When now-retired Cornell University President Frank Rhodes was a dean at Michigan, he was a highly sought-after speaker. Rhodes treated each alumni audience as something special. He didn't simply pull a well-traveled speech off the shelf. He believed that each audience deserved some insight that was just for them.

However, he had additional dimensions that alumni came to know and love. For example, on an alumni program in Switzerland, he spoke one evening on the creation of the Alps. As a geologist, he regaled the audience with the role of plate tectonics in creating the Alps. (Forgive me, Dr. Rhodes, there was more to it than that.)

However, what also stood out in the minds of alumni was that the next morning the group was to have their luggage outside their rooms by 5 a.m. (Now any alumni director will tell you that in the absence of bellhops and porters, alumni directors tote luggage down elevators and stairs.) As a colleague and I began moving a hundred pieces of luggage, there was Frank Rhodes carrying bags down the hallway at 5 a.m.—not just his bags, but everyone else's on his floor.

Rhodes was a great president at Cornell; but, he will be remembered by many Michigan alumni as an outstanding academic, administrator and a damn good bellhop.

At Michigan, the Faculty Senate elects a faculty member to the alumni association board of directors. It is just another way of developing symbiotic relationships between faculty and alumni. As alumni director, I was asked to speak at faculty assemblies. It was an opportunity to both thank them for their support of alumni activities and to bring them up to date on the ways alumni were supporting the needs of the faculty.

It always has been interesting to observe how men and women who have achieved great success in their lives will still stand in awe of their former professors. Captains of industry can be reduced to quaking undergraduates in the presence of "old" professor so and so, who taught them accounting 30 years ago.

Students become alumni. Alumni directors need to understand that to enable students to become participating alumni, they need to be treated as such from the day of their matriculation.

At Michigan, the alumni director was traditionally part of the freshmen convocation. The director's purpose was not only to welcome them as students but to emphasize that they were beginning a life-long journey that would link them to the university, and that the linkage would be "their" alumni association.

Student alumni councils are found in most alumni associations. The students are used as speakers and panelists at alumni functions, host alumni activities, organize parents' weekends, work in alumni offices, conduct tours for visitors and are involved in a myriad of other activities. Again, if one is mesmerized by numbers, student alumni organizations often fail any quantitative measurement as a percentage of the student body; however, those students who become involved as undergraduates become the alumni leaders of the future.

Relationships with university administrations take many forms. Regardless of the organizational approach used at your university, the alumni director needs to think of himself or herself as the representative of the university's largest and most influential constituency. Whether as a subordinate to a vice president of development or a member of the president's council or as the leader of an independent alumni association, one's relationship with the university administration and governing boards starts with one's self-image.

There is no way that any administrator at the decision-making level will take you seriously unless you take yourself seriously. Whether a president, vice president or dean, much of what they wish to accomplish for their university is vested in alumni support. Fund-raising, public support, community acceptance and awareness, student recruitment and political support are all aspects of university dependence upon alumni leadership and support. If alumni leaders see you as the focal point in their relationship with the university, then you have won half of the battle. The other half comes when administrators see you in the same manner.

Is all of this simply an ego-building process for an alumni director, or does it have a legitimate place in the well-being of the university? Each of the aspects of alumni support that I have mentioned does not require the massive participation of alumni, but rather careful leadership cultivation, training and development.

The importance of not falling victim to numbers cannot be over-stressed. If you are selling products, numbers are important. If you are assuming the role of director of development, numbers are important. But if you are trying to enable alumni to assume a rightful role in university governance and support, the answer is quality leadership.

If you are attempting to build a better relationship with the university president, begin by seeing yourself as a confidant and consultant on matters of alumni support.

If you sincerely believe in the values of education, it would behoove you to attend or audit classes. Doing so reminds us of what a university is all about. Faculty members will appreciate your continued interest in learning; and it refreshes your understanding of the role of students.

Attend conferences and symposia on campus. Write articles for other campus publications. Create op-ed pieces for newspapers. Speak at service clubs and community organizations. Be involved in community affairs as a volunteer leader. You are not only a leader in the university community but a major contributor to the local community and a champion of causes that benefit local citizens.

Perhaps the best thing that one can do to build relationships is to be informed. Be able to communicate with other campus leaders on matters of interest to them. Read the publications of faculty members. Attend the talks given by the president and follow the issues before the faculty senate or student government. Attend the meetings of trustees and regents and be prepared by studying the agenda as if you might be called upon to offer advice.

Universities may have a pecking order easily discerned on an organization chart. However, in a community that prides itself on its collegiality, relationships can simply be predicated on friendships. Athletic directors, vice presidents, deans, coaches, trustees, presidents, and faculty are all people who have personalities, virtues and values that make them good friends. Camaraderie and fellowship based on genuine fondness and respect adds immeasurably to one's personal life and allows for better understanding in working relationships.

SOCRATES ONCE SAID,

"I WOULD HAVE GIVEN MORE THOUGHT TO MY UTTERANCES IF I HAD KNOWN THAT PLATO WAS WRITING EVERYTHING DOWN."

REFLECTIONS

The Association of Alumni Secretaries was founded in 1913. As mentioned earlier, it was the forerunner to the American Alumni Council (AAC), which later with the American College Public Relations Association (ACPRA) became the Council for the Advancement and Support of Education (CASE).

In 1917, the organization published a handbook that should be required reading for every alumni professional. The following paragraphs are from the opening chapter of the handbook entitled "A Short Survey of Alumni Organization."

"Alumni organization in American colleges and universities is a comparatively recent development. Though the graduates of the earlier American colleges had a certain influence on the policies and growth of their alma mater, it is only within the last twenty-five years that these organizations have become a factor of any great importance.

In fact, this development is so recent that its significance is not sufficiently realized, least of all perhaps by the alumni themselves. When it is considered how vitally alumni influence enters into the life of our colleges and universities at the present time, the small space devoted to these organizations in most university histories and works on higher education in America is significant. It suggests at least just how much of a departure from those long educational precedents which lie behind our college system, is this habit of graduates to organize for fellowship and for the good of their respective institutions.

The desire to perpetuate college friendships and to revive memories of college days was undoubtedly the underlying cause, which first brought the alumni together in these organizations, and not a few associations have progressed no further in their activities. Gradually, however, the alumni organization came to play a more important part in the development of the college.

Nothing was more natural than for the authorities to look to the successful alumni when adding to the membership of its governing board, and just as naturally the organization of the alumni, either directly or indirectly, and almost invariably after a struggle with established customs, furnished the machinery for making the selection. The college authorities also came to recognize other possibilities for alumni association.

Use was made of them in securing financial assistance in the form of endowments and alumni funds, new buildings and equipment. Their aid was also invoked in efforts to increase the attendance. Thus it has come about that while the alumni have come to take an ever increasingly important part in the life of the institution, the chief direction of such activity has come from the administration, and the chief executive alumni officer has been very often a paid officer of the institution.

It is only recently that the alumni have organized, not as an adjunct of the college administration, but as a body designed to formulate independent alumni opinion, and to make intelligent alumni sentiment really effective for the good of the institution. With this new phase of alumni activity came new elements—the alumni-paid secretary, and the alumni journal. Practically every college or university in this country now has some sort of an alumni publication, either weekly, monthly or quarterly, designed to keep the graduates informed of the progress of their institution.

All the larger institutions and many of the smaller ones also have an officer who devotes all or at least a part of his time to the work."

Later in the opening chapter of the handbook, the authors quote from a speech given by Wilfred Shaw, alumni secretary of the University of Michigan. Shaw's speech was given at the fifth annual meeting of the Association of Alumni Secretaries. Reading it nearly 90 years later, I am impressed with two major aspects of the quotes from Shaw's talk: how much of what he said is germane to today's alumni world, and how well he expressed these views. In fact, in reading the various publications from the Association of Alumni Secretaries, one is struck with the eloquence of the written word and reminded of the fact that many of the early leaders were chosen because of their writing skills. Quoting Shaw:

"It is all very different now, the seeds sown in the first half of the nineteenth century are bearing fruit in this first half of the twentieth. This very meeting of accredited Alumni representatives is in itself a sufficient evidence of this new influence at work in American university life.

There is hardly an American college or university of any standing that does not have some sort of an alumni organization. Most of them have an officer whose duty it is to look after the interests of the alumni. The very fact that alumni have interests aside from the interests of their Alma Mater is in itself significant.

We are here to study the various problems, which have arisen between the college and its graduates. Our very presence is an acknowledgement of the vitality and the desirability of alumni influence, yet it seems fair to examine this movement and to endeavor to see as far as it is possible to do so, where and how far the movement we are engaged in may carry us.

It is generally recognized that all American colleges and universities are in a period of transition. The old day of the narrow humanistic curriculum has passed forever; everywhere we are entering broader educational fields and the process of adjustment, with its infinite number of questions is in full swing, and every institution is answering the requirements of the situation in its own way. Just at present there is no typical American university, but it is safe to predict that perhaps, at no great distance in the future, from this present era of individualism there will emerge several types of educational institutions, which will become standard all over the country.

The great part the alumni are to play in the direction of the colleges and universities of the future is the question we are more or less unconsciously, perhaps, hammering out right now. It is certain that the voice of the alumni is going to increase in influence in university councils in the future. Even now in universities what the alumni wish has often become the deciding factor in shaping educational policies.

Their support, sometimes advisory, sometimes financial, and sometimes political, gives to the alumni voice a weight which sometimes carries over that of the administrative officers and the faculty. There is no reason to believe that this influence will not continue to grow; we all know that the graduates of our universities have by no means accomplished all that they might for their institutions. To judge by the standards of what has been done by bodies of alumni in different universities, the possibilities of alumni activity seem almost unlimited.

Here lies a great element of strength and at the same time a weakness in our educational system. Here is a problem which we must recognize as alumni officers working both for the interests of our Alma Mater and for the alumni, fundamental in all the questions with which we are called upon to deal in the course of our various duties. We are at the focal point of a mighty force in the life of our colleges and universities.

It is only here and there in a speech by some college president that the significance of this movement is set forth. Anything which limits the progress of the institutions we represent, we must all acknowledge is a serious matter. It is quite conceivable that in building up an engine of such tremendous power as the alumni influence may well become, we are forging a two-edged sword.

We must understand that every alumni undertaking is not necessarily good because the alumni are behind it, it is all too easy to adopt some such view, but if we are true to our highest obligations we must look to the ultimate result in the real good of our institutions.

One of the great charms of the older English universities is the life which goes on in the ancient ivy covered quadrangles of the colleges preserved by traditions, handed down through numberless student generations. But those very quadrangles breathe a conservatism which is acknowledged to be one of the great defects of many of the English universities, a conservatism which is insisted upon by the graduates, or Convocation, in face of all attempts at reform.

The same restraining influence is sometimes laid upon progress in American universities; in effect it is said, let no hand be laid upon the customs or curriculum or buildings of one's own student days. Sometimes it is the other way, too, with us. New and radical ideas are launched upon alumni initiative without proper consideration; when they fail, and this is important, it is the university and not the alumni body which suffers.

These of course are extreme, some of the wisest and most progressive movements in our American universities have come as the result of alumni initiative. This, of course, is the ideal before us. The interest and the intelligent support of our alumni is one of the greatest sources of strength in our colleges and universities. It is our duty and our privilege to see that this support is stimulated in every possible way, but also to make sure that it is exerted in ways and through channels that make for the ultimate good of our institutions.

It is sometimes difficult to perceive in the glamour of the immediate and the obvious the wise course to take, but that is the duty laid upon us. So let me suggest, that in considering all the questions which we find before us on our program and which form the very warp and woof of our work, let us not forget the utility and beauty of the completed fabric. "

I am not certain what "warp and woof" means, but it is easy to feel great pride in Shaw's writing and his historical association with the University of Michigan. We can learn a lot from our predecessors. They are a reminder that we can legitimately claim that we are professionals, not hucksters or technicians.

•••

SOCRATES ONCE SAID,

"BE CAREFUL WHAT YOU WRITE, FOR WHEN YOU ARE GONE SOMEONE MIGHT JUST READ IT AND REALIZE THAT YOU WERE NOT AS SMART AS THEY REMEMBERED."

SOME THINGS REMEMBERED

The written word can be a useful tool in communicating one's thoughts and opinions. As an editorial or op-ed piece in an alumni magazine, it conveys to alumni your view on campus happenings or even wider observations on issues of major import. One of the most rewarding letters I ever received was from an alumna who was a high school history teacher. She wrote that she posted each of my "Moments for Michigan" editorials on her classroom bulletin board.

Thanks to Michigan Alumni President Steve Grafton and the Michigan Alumnus Magazine, I have reprinted several editorials written in the late 1980s and early 1990s. Frankly, I simply reached into a box of bound

•••

magazines and pulled out several editions. They are not the worst nor the best of 28 years of writing editorials. However, they are representative of matters that I deemed worthy of sharing with alumni.

Selected at random, the topics show the wide range of interests that an alumni director can share with the alumni audience. Signed editorials or op-ed pieces reflect a personal opinion and reinforce the alumni concept that "their" person on campus is sharing his or her views on issues of importance.

This editorial dealt with a tax proposal with a direct effect on public support of higher education.

A MOMENT FOR MICHIGAN
SEPTEMBER 1984

Proposal C, which will appear on the state of Michigan's November election ballot, is better known within the state as "Voter's Choice." The proposal calls for an amendment to Article 9 of the state's constitution.

Basically, the proposed change would require a popular vote on the adoption of any new tax or any legislative changes in the base or rate of a state or local tax, if such changes result in an increase in revenue. It would also require that increases in state or local fees, licenses, permits, etc. be approved either by a 4/5 vote of the appropriate governing body or by a majority of voters in an election. I would make the above requirements retroactive to 31 December 1981. In addition, it would prohibit local non-resident income tax rates of more than .05 per cent and, finally, it would require that ballot proposals on tax questions must state the total anticipated revenue, the intended use of the revenues, and the expiration date.

It is a proposal that at first view may seem attractive to many taxpayers. The burden of government support exerts tremendous pressure on already strained personal finances. Even the most conscientious citizens might view the proposal as providing relief and, at the same time, allowing for subsequent redress as various proposals are individually voted upon in the future.

However, the effects of such a proposal are both immediate and long term. The Citizens Research Council of Michigan estimates the rollback provision would decrease state revenues by $630 million in fiscal year 1985, although it would take effect for only the remaining eight months of that fiscal year. In subsequent years, it would amount to $946 million – nearly one billion dollars – on an annual basis. The council also suggests that, if unemployment compensations are to be included, an additional $537 million loss would result.

For higher education, Proposal C threatens cutbacks which could be devastating. It is estimated that the rollback to 1981 levels could force Michigan's four-year colleges and universities to lose about $67 million annually and the two-year community colleges would lose at least $28 million. Such reductions would again place a disproportionate burden for financing education on students and their families.

Wayne State University has indicated that it would have to raise its tuition by at least 23 percent to compensate for projected revenue shortfall. That increase, in turn, might have to be approved by the voters under the language of Proposal C. The

U-M Board of Regents addresses the concerns of this University in a statement on page 9.

The ramifications of Proposal C are even more disturbing when one considers that every revenue tax program throughout the state – school district, cities, and governmental units at all levels – would have to seek immediate voter approval to meet even minimal service needs.

Proponents of "Voter's Choice" may, indeed, be dedicated supporters of public education and may, in truth, feel that specific revenue issues supporting public education would be approved at later dates. However, the sheer enormity of organizing such elections, the expense of campaigning, and the probable lack of public interest with such elections would make shambles out of even the best intentioned tax reform program. It is likely that only those wishing to "vote no" would turn out for such elections in large proportions.

We are a nation founded on the principles of representative government. We elect people to manage our public resources and provide basic services. We monitor their performance at regular intervals through the election process. In addition, we have other recourses: we have the rights of recall and initiative, which provide the public with the opportunity to overturn legislative decisions or to substitute their own judgments for those of others.

Michigan is a state that in recent years has under funded the needs of public education, not necessarily because of the will or desire of those in the governmental process but because economic factors have so dictated. The economic recovery in the state and the positive attitude of state officials toward the proper support of education is, indeed, placed in jeopardy by the "Voter's Choice" proposal known as Proposal C.

Finally, we must examine what we really want in our society. Fundamentally, I believe all responsible citizens desire that government provide the services necessary to educate our people, protect our citizenry, and care for the health and welfare of our people.

To maintain a University of distinction, one that continues to contribute to both the quality of life of individuals and the needs of society, requires that we make our own voter's choice.

Yours for Michigan,
Bob Forman

This editorial dealt with nuclear warfare, a topic as germane today as twenty-three years ago.

A MOMENT FOR MICHIGAN
JANUARY 1985

This issue of Michigan Alumnus presents observations by University of Michigan faculty and alumni on subjects relating to our national security, nuclear arms, and disarmament. The articles were written to enhance our general understanding of these paramount issues facing the world today. Because of the comprehensive nature of this subject, we have extended the normal length of this magazine by combining our January and February issues.

In his excellent article, James A. Blight quotes a letter from a 10-year-old child written to President Reagan. "I don't want to die," wrote the child, "I don't want my family to die." The child concluded by asking the president to, "Please stop the nuclear bombs." Blight goes on to report that the majority of Americans believe "it is only a matter of time" before nuclear weapons are used unless we have new and creative approaches to avoid such a catastrophe.

It is safe to assume that no one, Soviet or American, wished to die from the blast or after-effects of a nuclear bomb. It is not surprising that opinion polls and surveys tell us that. What is astonishing is that in spite of the well-documented fear of nuclear war, the intensity of commitment to avoid such a catastrophe seems nearly non-existent. There are protest movements, political statements, writings, and great trooping back and forth with respect to nuclear warfare. Yet most of the world seems strangely indifferent to the prospect of such an eventuality.

Forty years ago, the United States exploded two nuclear bombs in cities with largely civilian populations. In Hiroshima alone, 130,000 of its 350,000 inhabitants died from the bomb's effects. The bombings were not the irrational actions of a ruthless dictator. They were the considered decisions of scientific, political, and military leaders, based on rational assessments.

In 1945 there were people in this country, largely but not exclusively among the scientific community, who argued the immorality of the use of the bomb. They raised concerns that not only did the weapons indiscriminately kill young and old, civilian and military alike, but they had the uncertain potential of destroying all life on earth.

We are now engaged in a massive build-up of nuclear arms and the delivery systems necessary to place them on target. The major world powers have predicated their nuclear strategies on the principle of deterrence. Simply stated, we are telling each other that we will immediately retaliate in kind. To reinforce this point, both par-

ROBERT FORMAN ▣ 93

ties continue to improve their capabilities to deliver nuclear warheads to each other's principal military and civilian targets.

The difficulty of deterrence as a strategy for maintaining peace is that it assumes that the participants will always behave rationally in a crisis situation. Furthermore, it assumes that your opponent will believe you are capable of retaliating or will even fear that you will strike first if sufficiently provoked. It is a strategy based on the assumption that, caught in a world crisis, leaders will act rationally and reasonably. This seems to totally disregard world history.

Most people have learned that seldom is human conduct successfully managed by deterrence. Misbehaving children caught up in the emotions of a given moment are frequently not constrained by the thought of parental discipline. Societal threats of death or incarceration seem limited with respect to stopping or preventing criminal activity.

We are a nation confused, concerned, and divided on these subjects. These divisions are even more disturbing because we not only have varying perceptions of which strategies we should pursue, but a great many of us lack either a true understanding of our circumstances or, more tragically, simply do not care.

A commonality we all possess, however, is hope. We believe that most people would not wish a nuclear death upon our fellow humans or ourselves, yet civilization witnesses' murder and brutality as commonplace. We know that human beings have historically resolved conflict by physical and armed aggression, yet we cling to a hope that the very awesomeness of nuclear war will prevent us from falling victim to it.

Mankind needs to place its hopes on something more positive than fear. We must assume that the strategies of the moment are merely holding actions which allow more time to permit us to develop a quality of human behavior matching our technological knowledge.

In truth, our fears are not of nuclear weapons but of people. Our hopes lie also in people and their willingness to grasp the difference between "love thy neighbor" and "an eye for an eye."

Yours for Michigan,
Bob Forman

This editorial dealt with the quality of American education.

A MOMENT FOR MICHIGAN
MARCH 1985

Few people doubt the importance of education to American society. It is the cornerstone of our democratic system and essential to the quality of our lives. Yet while every public opinion poll taken on the subject lends credence to this observation, it seems that there is much to worry about as we examine our educational system as a whole. Whether it be an analysis of what is wrong with our elementary or secondary schools or a review of our higher educational programs, there seems to be a nationwide assessment that much is lacking.

The National Commission on Excellence in Education, in its much heralded report of April 1983, lamented the condition of education by making a number of sobering observations, a few of which are listed here:

- Some 23 million American adults are functionally illiterate by the simplest tests of everyday reading, writing, and comprehension.

- About 13 percent of all seventeen-year-olds in the United States can be considered to be functionally illiterate. Functional illiteracy among minority youth may run as high as 40 percent.

- The College Board's Scholastic Aptitude Tests demonstrate a virtually unbroken decline from 1963 to 1980. Average verbal scores fell more than 50 points and average mathematics scores dropped nearly 40 points.

- Average achievement of high school students on most standardized tests is now lower than 26 years ago when Sputnik was launched.

- Many seventeen-year-olds do not possess the "higher order" intellectual skills we should expect of them. Nearly 40 percent can draw inferences from written material; only one-fifth can write a persuasive essay and only one-third can solve a mathematics problem requiring several steps.

- Between 1980 and 1985 remedial mathematics courses in public four-year colleges increased by 72 percent and now constitute one-quarter of all mathematics courses taught in those institutions.

- Business and military leaders complain that they are required to spend millions of dollars on costly remedial education and training programs in such basic skills as reading, writing, spelling, and computation. The Department of the Navy, for example, reported to the commission that one-quarter of its recent recruits cannot read at the ninth grade level, the minimum needed simply to understand written safety instructions. Without remedial work they cannot even begin, much less complete, the sophisticated training essential in much of the modern military.

While there are many doomsday proposals for education today, as I suspect there always have been, we should not take their challenges lightly, for they have a profound effect on all of us.

Despite this plethora of negative studies and observations, there is evidence of a major awakening among both the practitioners in the field of education and the public at large, calling for immediate and aggressive action.

This issue of Michigan Alumnus presents some of the innovative and creative programs being developed by our School of Education, particularly those utilizing computers and modern technology. The school has come to an early understanding not only of the importance of education to a world dependent economically, socially, and politically upon technological advancements, but also that the same technology can provide the basis for new and imaginative teaching tools.

Dean Carl Berger and his colleagues have created a new vitality in the School of Education, striving for goals that are the worthy partners of those of our other distinguished schools. Michigan's leadership tradition in teaching, research, and public service seems readily apparent in the current efforts of the School of Education.

Yours for Michigan,
Bob Forman

A MOMENT FOR MICHIGAN
SEPTEMBER 1985

For the first time in more than a decade, the state legislature has appropriated a generous increase in funding to higher education. This was a difficult decision for the lawmakers of a state that continues to deal with numerous economic concerns and it is to their credit that they perceived and acted upon the importance of higher education as reflected in their funding for fiscal 1985-86.

Recognizing the significance of the current appropriation, Governor James Blanchard requested that all of Michigan's state-assisted schools freeze 1985-86 tuition for in-state students. In response to that request, the administration and regents of The University of Michigan made an equally difficult decision and, for the second year in a row, froze in-state tuition.

It should be understood that no one at the University wishes to increase the financial burden on students and their families with respect to tuition. However, as one of a very few publicly assisted universities that offers an education that is competitive with that offered by the major private institutions of this country, Michigan has a unique set of needs in order to maintain the educational, research, and public service programs at the level of quality which the University has traditionally offered its students and its state.

In his recent book, The Public Ivys, Richard Moll, dean of admissions at the University of California at Santa Cruz, guides his readers on a tour of the state-supported colleges and universities that have long been recognized for their educational quality. Michigan's own tradition of excellence is attested to by Moll who refers to the University as "the prototype Public Ivy." Later, he notes:

Appearances may disappoint and Michigan may not have the instant Ivy aura of the University of Virginia or William and Mary. But its history, tradition, and noteworthy accomplishments through the decades caused Clark Kerr, former president of the University of California and chairman of the Carnegie Commission of Higher Education, to say: "The University of Michigan has fully earned its credit as 'mother of state universities'."

Kerr told a Michigan commencement audience that Michigan first demonstrated that a state university could achieve high academic quality.

That The University of Michigan is a unique leader among both private and public institutions of higher education is underscored by Moll, who lists some of the University's recorded firsts. Included among these are that The University of Michigan was first: to de-emphasize the classical college curriculum and sponsor such "new" studies as the sciences and modern languages; to entirely own and operate a hospital; to offer instruction in journalism; to provide instruction in aeronautical engineering; and to offer a program in nuclear engineering.

Moll's point in taking these introspective looks at Michigan and the other "Public Ivys" is explained in the introduction of his book when he points to the growing trend of students who are accepted for admission to the most costly private universities, yet more and more often select the less expensive public institution of similar quality and rising prestige. "America enjoys a wealth of variety in higher education," he writes. "But the top of the private sector has typically been the best and the most prestigious. The naming of the Public Ivys belatedly begs for a turning point in that tradition. This 'other sector' has come fully of age—although the quality has often been there, public perception has not matched it."

In this same vein, I would like to urge each of us, the alumnae and alumni of the University, and the people and legislators of the state of Michigan, to rekindle our own self-perceptions of what it means to be a university that is both premier and publicly supported.

The University of Michigan possesses a unique character and quality among public universities. In it, the state of Michigan has an asset that ranks among its major resources, if not its most important. We cannot afford to diminish the quality that has distinguished this great institution.

The University's willingness to support the governor's request for an in-state tuition freeze is in keeping with its long-standing commitment to excellence and accessibility. The decision on the part of Gov. Blanchard and the state legislature to strengthen the state's support to its public institutions is a positive beginning. But it is only through continued public support in the future that this prototype Public Ivy can itself continue to provide its state and its students with the quality teaching, research, and public-service programs that have characterized its proud and unique history.

Yours for Michigan,
Bob Forman

• •

An editorial praising the work of staff colleagues and their contribution to the work of the association.)

A MOMENT FOR MICHIGAN
MAY 1986

This magazine has many objectives to meet and roles to perform. Its feature articles provide insight into a variety of topics which affect each of our lives. At the same time, its departments keep you informed about major events at the University as well as various matters which related to the Alumni Association itself – meetings, travel opportunities, enrichment programs, etc.

In doing all of this, we sometimes neglect to mention the contributions of individuals that make this Alumni Association the type of organization that it is. Through the years we have been fortunate to have been judged by peer organizations across the country as one of the foremost independent alumni associations in the United States.

Frequently I have called to your attention the role played by alumni volunteer leadership in making this possible. In addition, we have been blessed by the commitment and competency of a dedicated professional staff. For example, in the last year, two men who have spent a lifetime in service to the Alumni Association have retired – Harold Wilson, '42, who worked for the Alumni Association over thirty-eight years, and Bill Stegath, '42,' M.A. '49, Ph.D. '61, whose contributions extended over twenty-three years.

Over the course of their professional careers at the Alumni Association, Hal and Bill held nearly all of the important positions of staff responsibility. Recently, the Council for the Advancement and Support of Education honored both men at its district conference in Chicago.

Hal, who received his degree in journalism and was sports editor of the Michigan Daily, joined the Alumni Association in 1947 and was managing editor of Michigan Alumnus for thirteen years during the 1950s and early 1960s. He coordinated reunion and constituent societies' activities, assisted in the development of the family camping program and, as director of the association's alumni travel program, developed and expanded that area into one of the largest and most comprehensive of any U.S. university. Hal also served for many years as the associate executive director of the association.

Before joining the Alumni Association in 1962, Bill was a faculty member of U-M's speech department and on the staff of University radio station WUOM, where his productions won eight national awards. He is well-known to area radio audiences as the half-time host on Detroit radio station WJR during the U-M football season. He has served the Alumni Association in various capacities including the alumni club program, the alumni enrichment program, and as the first director of Camp Michigan-Walloon. He has also been affiliated with the Swiss camp program for most of the fifteen years since its inception. Bill concluded his career with the association as an assistant executive director.

Hal and Bill share the same class year at Michigan – 1942 – and have worn their loyalty, allegiance, and commitment to this University on their sleeves, for everyone to observe. Neither are persons who limited their contributions to forty-hour weeks. Scarcely a weekend or an evening would go by that you would not find them at the office or involved in some other alumni activity. Through the years they came to know literally thousands of alumni on a first-name basis.

In some ways it is a disadvantage for them to be coupled in this essay, for they both need the separate recognition and distinction that their individual contributions warrant. Yet, since so much of their professional careers and their college days were spent together, I am certain that they will not object to my writing of them in tandem.

Personally, I am grateful that both Hal and Bill continue to reside in the Ann Arbor area and are frequent visitors to the Alumni Association. Their friendship and presence are highly valued by all members of our staff, and their contributions to our ongoing activities remain as helpful today in their retirement as it was during their days of active employment.

I know that I speak for all of you who have come in contact with these two outstanding persons through the years, and I know that you would want me to wish them a long and happy retirement and grateful thanks for jobs well done.

Yours for Michigan,
Bob Forman

A view of American diversity and immigration

A MOMENT FOR MICHIGAN
JULY 1986

I read the article written by August C. Bolino in this issue of Michigan Alumnus with considerable personal interest. My ancestors came to this country for many of the reasons that Professor Bolino so aptly describes. In fact, one of his illustrations so nearly fits my paternal grandfather that I looked again to see if the initials used in the example were not his.

As I indicated in the March/April issue of this magazine, we are a nation that differs in many ways from the country that welcomed so many immigrants through the processes of Ellis Island.

We are a nation of people from varied racial and cultural backgrounds. We are not nearly as geographically limited as those who earlier passed through the portals of Ellis Island. Yet, the reasons for coming remain the same: discontent and despair, with the hope and aspiration for greater opportunities in a new land.

Immigration is often difficult for us to comprehend. We are a country, with the exception of our Native American population, that can trace its roots to a multitude of foreign origins. Thus we owe our very existence to the generosity of prior immigration policies, excepting, of course, those Americans whose ancestors were brought here as part of the abhorrent slave trade.

Yet, we find ourselves confronted with our own self-interest. We question whether the opportunities provided our forefathers should be extended to a new generation of people who suffer from the same injustices or disadvantages that prompted so many of our ancestors to seek a new haven in America. Displaced persons, people suffering from tyrannical governments, those disadvantaged by unworkable economic systems – all seek refuge in our republic. Yet we know our own nation to have its own disadvantaged peoples, and we often find our views in conflict as we recognize our need to solve internal problems as well as to provide for others.

It was a less demanding test for America to become one of the world's great nations when there was an abundance of natural resources, available land, and cheap labor. However, the real challenge comes in attempting to make this nation responsive to new generations of people in need when such conditions no longer exist.

Many new Americans may never see the Statue of Liberty, but their aspirations are the same as those of previous generations. Immigrants will come from Latin America, Southeast Asia, and other places where political freedom may be denied or economic opportunity nonexistent. This nation must work for all such peoples in the way that it once worked for largely European immigrants.

We have become, as one writer says, less a melting pot and more a garden salad – a population of minorities with differing cultural heritages, languages, social and economic backgrounds, but with common aspirations.

Emma Lazarus' poem about the Statue of Liberty is as valid today as it was in the past:

Give me you tired, your poor,

Your huddled masses, yearning to breathe free,

The wretched refuse of your teeming shore,

Send these, the homeless, tempest-tossed, to me,

I lift my lamp beside the golden door.

Yours for Michigan,
Bob Forman

● ●

*An article responding to major appropriation cutbacks
and the University's autonomy.)*

A MOMENT FOR MICHIGAN
SEPTEMBER 1988

Michigan Governor James Blanchard has, for several years, championed the cause of lower tuitions for state-assisted universities. One cannot fault the governor's desire to limit the costs of education for students and their families.

This year, The University of Michigan received the lowest percentage increase among the state's 15 public universities. This is the third straight year that the University has been at the low end of public support.

The governor and the legislature have a difficult task. The demands for state appropriations come from every area of public interest. To attempt to satisfy all of those interests with limited resources is, of course, an ongoing challenge for public officials.

The Regents of The University of Michigan are a constitutionally autonomous body. They operate under a distinct mandate of the people of the state and are directly responsible to them. They have both the authority and the responsibility for assuring the quality and the performance of The University of Michigan.

This year, because of the inadequacy of state appropriations, the Regents elected to increase tuition by 12 percent. Their approach was basically the same as other public universities in the state. The governor promptly called for a rollback in these tuition proposals and ultimately the institutions acquiesced. The proposed 1988-89 tuition and registration fee increases at the U-M currently stands at just under 10 percent for in-state undergraduate students.

The University is a great educational enterprise. It has not attained that status by accident. For 150 years, it has profited by public recognition of the tremendous asset it provides to the state and its people. It is consistently ranked among the highest quality universities in this country.

The value of this ranking is not that it gives the University community a reason for pride, but that it presents a unique opportunity for quality education to students of this state, obtainable in only a handful of public and private universities.

In many ways, The University of Michigan may be the state's greatest single sustaining asset. Not only does the University educate and prepare professional business and educational leaders, but it also provides the research and service that offers the state continuing hope for a growing and expanding economy.

Whether it is one's family, business, or an educational enterprise, when expense exceeds income, there must be some prioritization and cutbacks. It should be remembered that The University of Michigan has undertaken just such action throughout the 1980's – reducing the expenditure in several schools and colleges, prioritizing its work, and undergoing across-the-board budgetary cuts. In fact, its efforts in this regard have been used as a model for other institutions of higher education.

No one at the University wishes to have students and their families pay a larger share of the financial burden for operating this institution. In recent years the University has developed an extensive program for private support from its alumni and friends. It has done those things which are prudent and wise to reduce costs and maintain quality during times of extraordinary financial burdens.

The Regents raised tuition only as a last resort, and even then they were not unanimous in their decision. University officials who agreed to the governor's demands for a rollback may have made the only appropriate choice, given the political consequences involved. The entire situation, however, imperils our great University. Students who come to The University of Michigan expect a quality education. It profits them little to diminish the quality of their education by paying less for it. Michigan's tuition is, and always has been, high relative to other state-assisted schools. That, in part, is the cost of quality.

The University has taken extraordinary means to assure financial assistance to those students with demonstrated need. This assistance package, including outright grants, loans and work-study programs, has virtually assured all in-state students that their financial needs at The University of Michigan can be met. In fact, a sizeable portion of the original, proposed tuition increases had been designated for student financial assistance.

For 150 years, the University has prospered by its autonomy and by partnership with state government with regard to its public support. If this situation should cease to exist, the losers will not be the politicians and the Regents, but the people of Michigan.

Great assets are built over long periods of time and, once impaired or destroyed, are nearly impossible to reestablish.

Yours for Michigan,
Bob Forman

An editorial that combined an historic University event with the more modern introduction of a new University president and his wife.

A MOMENT FOR MICHIGAN
JANUARY 1989

Ah, the wonders of technology...

It was heralded as the event that would "send the spirit of Michigan abroad in the land," and indeed it did. On 29 April 1922, the first Michigan "Reunion by Radio" program was broadcast throughout the nation by the Detroit News radio station WWJ, bringing together small groups of alumni in cities on both coasts and across the Midwest.

It was, by all accounts, a gala affair. According to the Michigan Alumnus of 14 May 1922: "The programme opened the 'The Victors' as played by the University Band. Then the Glee Club sang 'Laudes Atque Carmina', ''Tis of Michigan We sing,' and 'I want to Go Back to Michigan.' 'Duke' Dunne, captain of the 1921 football team spoke on the Boosters Club.

Then the University Banjo Quintet played a number of selections. Carl Johnson, secretary of the University of Michigan Club of Detroit, spoke on the need of keeping alumni alive and working for Michigan. Judge William M. Heston, better known as 'Willie', spoke reminiscently of the days when he was in school. He also declared that Michigan has three points of superiority over all other universities: her President, her athletic head, and her loyal alumni body."

There were more speeches, by other august persons: Fielding H. Yost, director of athletics, spoke of the University's place in athletics, pointing out Olympic athletes, world records, and All-Americans; President Marion Burton appealed to alumni for their continuing support in his "The Greater Michigan" address. The grand finale was the Glee Club performance of "The Yellow and the Blue."

Response to the "programme" was enthusiastic. "The best estimate possible puts at 25,000 the number of alumni that 'listened in' on the Radio Reunion program.... Such figures put the imagination to rout," said the Michigan Alumnus, and letters from alumni listeners echoed the impression the broadcast has made.

"Three Michigan alumni of this city attended and listened in on Michigan's Radio Reunion...and were wonderfully surprised as well as immensely delighted with the two hours' programme," wrote Sanford Trippet, '04, of Princeton, Indiana. "We heard four speakers very plainly throughout their speeches...The banjos were probably the best heard of any numbers...It certainly thrilled us to be able to listen in."

"The programme proved very satisfactory here, the weather conditions being perfect. The musical numbers proved more successful than the speeches, although every word of President Burton's speech was plainly audible," wrote another correspondent from Lima, Ohio.

Perhaps, though, the true import of the broadcast was best summed up in a Michigan Alumnus editorial of May 11: "It is difficult to estimate how many alumni were thus brought into vital and almost personal touch with the University through the ether...the University (now) has a way of entering more closely than ever before into the life of the people of the state and the nation."

It is that "vital and almost personal touch" that we sometimes feel we have lost, here in the 1990's as the University's alumni body grows larger and we move easily, perhaps too easily, away from our roots, be they familial or educational. But the Michigan family always finds a way to be together, and the Alumni Association is pleased to announce another technological reunion.

On 9 April 1989, only 20 days short of 67 years since the 1922 broadcast, alumni throughout the country are invited to join us, via satellite, at the President's House on The University of Michigan's Ann Arbor campus for a very special program. President and Mrs. Duderstadt will be there to greet you. This is a wonderful opportunity to meet the new man and the helm of the University and hear firsthand his plans and his vision for this great institution. He would like to personally ask for your understanding, support, and guidance as our University strives to meet today's needs and tomorrow's challenges. As a special feature of the program, Anne Duderstadt will lead a tour through the President's House, the oldest building on campus.

This "reunion by satellite" will come to you through a series of concurrent club meetings which will be held in major cities throughout the country. Your local club leaders will act as hosts for the event, and you will receive notice of the specifics for the gathering well in advance of April 9.

This will indeed be a gathering of friends, for if I have learned one thing in the 25 years that I have worked for the Alumni Association it is that the alumni of Michigan look upon each other and this institution in the manner of family and friends. That family will be gathering on April 9. Please join us that day to visit with President and Mrs. Duderstadt, and help us once again "send the spirit of Michigan abroad in the land."

Yours for Michigan,
Bob Forman

....

Two University events with little in common,
yet representative of the values of the
University community.

A MOMENT FOR MICHIGAN
MARCH 1989

Two recent activities associated with our University community serve as a reminder of what a special place The University of Michigan is. Our Big Ten championship football team won the 1989 Rose Bowl, making the victors true "champions of the West." The 1,500 alumni who were part of the official alumni Rose Bowl tour were not only thrilled by the great victory over the University of Southern California, but also enjoyed a variety of quality programs.

A series of faculty lectures examined such topics as graduate education, the Peoples Republic of China, and innovations in the field of music. James Duderstadt, president of The University of Michigan, spoke to alumni groups on several occasions. In a New Year's Day address to more than 1,000 alumni, he discussed the University's commitment to diversity and the University as a paradigm for the research university of the twenty-first century.

A captivating band concert featured The University of Michigan Marching Band, and we were entertained by other student groups such as the Friars. At the venerable Hollywood Palladium, we honored Coach Bo Schembechler and his championship team and were regaled by Bob Hope and singer Rita Coolidge. Our West Coast alumni joined us at these events and were, of course, represented in large numbers at the game itself.

The opportunity for students, faculty, and alumni to attend events in California that were intellectual, entertaining, and exciting, created a very meaningful occasion for all of us. It was a happy, but tired throng that left the Rose Bowl Stadium proudly singing "The Victors."

As I write this message to you, another event is taking place on our campus. It may seem a peculiar contrast to Rose Bowl activities, but it is also a poignant moment in the history of our University. As is often stated in these pages, the University community has a strong and positive commitment to the development and practice of the values of diversity. The events commemorating the life of Martin Luther King, Jr., provided an extraordinary demonstration of this commitment.

In its recognition of Martin Luther King, Jr., Day, the University community not only remembered the life and work of this great American, but renewed its commitment to developing a University where Reverend King's dream might come closer to reality.

Students, faculty, and alumni came together in a series of events and meetings to enhance our understanding and demonstrate our commitment.

Willie Brown, speaker of the California State Assembly, provided a Hill Auditorium audience with special insights into the life of Dr. King. He spoke about King and reminded us that, if we are able to support our convictions with hard work and dedication, we need not be giants to accomplish important goals. His sensitive portrayal of Dr. King made members of the audience realize their own potential for accomplishment.

Members of the University community joined in a Unity March led by leaders of various student organizations and by President Duderstadt. Individual units of the campus conducted a variety of programs involving staff, faculty students, and alumni.

Our own alumni association staff, with association President Geraldine Ford and a large group of students, viewed a 20-year-old documentary film on the life of Martin Luther King, Jr. Afterward, we examined the impact of Dr. King's work upon our lives and the message that it sent. We then attempted to review the work of the alumni association with regard to promoting the principles of diversity in a pluralistic society. Student input to our deliberations was insightful and remarkable.

It was a moment when the very best of education was being realized. We were renewing our commitment and increasing our understanding. Similar stories could be told a hundred-fold across the University campus.

Andrew Young, mayor of Atlanta, Georgia, closed the formal program with a thoughtful and moving address.

Martin Luther King, Jr. Day and the University's observance of our commitment to diversity is, of course, not a singular event. The usefulness of that day set aside for education is only of value if the lessons learned continue to be a part of the ongoing life of the University community.

To share my thoughts with you on two disparate subjects such as the Martin Luther King, Jr. Day observances and the Rose Bowl, is not meant to suggest that these two events in any way equate with each other. However, the two activities remind us how fortunate we all are to be a part of the Michigan family.

Yours for Michigan,
Bob Forman

A piece dealing with the accomplishments of
Michigan's independent alumni association.

A MOMENT FOR MICHIGAN
SEPTEMBER 1991

As members of your independent Alumni Association, you are stockholders in the sense that it is your organization, and you have a decided proprietary interest in what is happening. I would like to share with you a kind of potpourri of events, happenings, and observations that I hope you will find relevant to your own interests in your association.

At the annual Alumni Luncheon, held Saturday, 8 June 1991, Verne G. Istock, '62, M.B.A. '63, who served the association and its members extraordinarily well, turned over the presidential gavel to his successor, Richard D. Rattner, 67, of Birmingham, Michigan.

Verne Istock understood the difference between policy and day-to-day operations. As president, his focus was chiefly as chairman of the Board of Directors of the Alumni Association and he made a number of important decisions during his tenure. Among them was the establishment of a strong alumni legislative advocacy program, which focuses on state support to education, and reminds public officials of the importance of education to Michigan residents – in terms of the quality of their lives as well as the economic growth and well-being of our statewide community. As a corporate executive, Verne understood the need for such an organized effort and was in the vanguard of its implementation.

There have been significant financial challenges to the association this past year. Our organization depends chiefly on membership income and other self-supporting entrepreneurial services, such as alumni travel, insurance, and camping programs. Due to the recession and Desert Storm, income from some of these sources was substantially diminished. However, we have been able to exercise prudent cost controls and energize other income resources to maintain the high level of institutional support that is our primary mission. Still in place are our programs in under-represented minority recruitment, scholar awards, emergency student aid, and continuing education, as well as the basic alumni programs offered in all of the schools and colleges, alumni clubs, reunions and, of course, our important communications vehicle, this magazine.

New this year was the implementation of an affinity credit card program under the auspices of the Alumni Association. Alumni associations across the country provide specially designed affinity cards that relate to their institutions. While such programs are not of the highest priority to us (in all candor, they are available through almost any local or national organization), we believed that the potential to provide badly needed resources for our programs of service to the University was one that we could no longer overlook.

As a Michigan banker, Verne Istock was sensitive to the competitive nature of such programs, and the fact that such a decision would not be totally acceptable to some people. Under his guidance, we conducted a blind review of both in-state and out-or-state bank programs. Our board's Alumni Services and Membership Benefits Committee voted on an appropriate bank, based on an objective evaluation of pre-determined criteria, without knowing which specific bank's program they were selecting. Only then was the bank, MBNA America (a Delaware bank), identified. Such decisions in a voluntary organization are difficult, time-consuming and challenging.

The implementation of a $2 million capital campaign to enhance facilities at Camp Michigania at Walloon Lake also occurred during Verne Istock's presidency. At this point, more than $1.2 million of that goal has been realized. Verne and his wife Judith Warnke Istock, '62ed, were co-chairmen of the Special Gifts Committee for the campaign and worked closely with still another former president of the Alumni Association, the overall chair of the campaign, Albert "Pete" Pickus, '53.

This spring, the association received a gold medal from the Council for the Advancement and Support of Education in the competition for best overall alumni relations program in America.

These are only a partial catalog of important decisions and happenings during Verne Istock's two-year term as president.

Having served as vice-president of the association, chairman of a number of important boards of directors committees, a member of the executive committee, past president of The University of Michigan Club of Greater Detroit and a recipient of that club's Distinguished Alumni Service Award, Rich Rattner brings demonstrated leadership experience to the presidency.

He inherits a continuing set of association challenges. Among them is our ability to maintain our independence through our financial viability and to make certain that our priorities of service to the University and to our fellow alumni and alumnae are constantly being reassessed and reevaluated.

Yours for Michigan,
Bob Forman

• •

An editorial concerning the role of the alumni in the
nominating process for the partisan election of
University Regents.

A MOMENT FOR MICHIGAN
MAY 1992

There are 85,000 members of the Alumni Association of the University of Michigan, all of whom have a high degree of motivation to serve the interests of their alma mater. For those alumni and alumnae living in the state of Michigan, there is no greater service than assuring that the regents – the University's governing board – be people with the highest degree of competence, vision, and motivation.

An effective Alumni Association is obligated to ask all people who share this desire for regental quality to encourage qualified candidates to seek nomination through the normal political process. It is important to note that your Alumni Association urges all of its members to actively participate in the political process, whether it is to support higher educational funding at the state or national level or to advocate quality leadership at the state level – gubernatorial, legislative, and regental.

At the U-M Board of Regents meeting in May, Regent Deane Baker expressed concern about the level of involvement of the Alumni Association in the selection of candidates for the U-M Board of Regents. He stated "that some regent's emeriti, all of whom are directors of the Alumni Association, have established themselves as a committee to recommend candidates for the office of regent to the Republican Party." He also stated that I had interviewed these prospective candidates, and that one individual had been referred to the governor's office "as a candidate satisfactory to the committee."

Regent Baker's statements are incorrect. The Alumni Association has no committee, either formally authorized or informally constituted. The four regent emeriti who are members of the 63-member national Alumni Association board of directors are persons who have had long-standing and significant relationships in the political processes of this state. Membership on our board of directors does not require disenfranchisement from the political process; political actions taken by individual board members are self-initiated and support their own convictions.

As to my own involvement, in the 26 years that I have been the executive director of the Alumni Association – and this year is no exception – people seeking nomination for the office of regent have chosen to meet with me. Their questions are basically the same: what do you believe alumni and alumnae feel are the priorities and challenges of the University, and what can I do to seek their support?

The priorities, I believe, are straightforward: alumni and alumnae want this University to maintain its quality, to guarantee access for qualified students regardless of their economic circumstances, to further the goals of this University in terms of diversity, and to continue to be an institution that serves the needs of the people of this state and prepares our students and, as a consequence, the state of Michigan, for involvement in a global society.

As to how to enlist the support of Michigan graduates, candidates should demonstrate that they possess the qualities of leadership necessary to implement the aforementioned goals.

Yours for Michigan,
Bob Forman

SOCRATES ONCE SAID,

"ALL HISTORY SEEMS TO BE WRITTEN ABOUT WAR. IT WOULD BE REMARKABLE IF THE SAME CHRONICLES WERE WRITTEN ABOUT PEACE."

WHAT IF?

Obviously alumni directors cannot orchestrate world peace. However, if world peace is ever obtained it will be through education. Let us dream of a time when peace replaces the Super Bowl, the World Series, the Final Four, Britney Spears, Tom Cruise and video games as the major concern of the civilized world. What if the ministers, mullahs, priests, monks, rabbis and all other religious leaders simply said "enough is enough?"

What if they concluded that God, Allah or Whomever must be terribly saddened and disappointed with all the killing and maiming done in His name? What if educated people began to realize that the use of force to reconcile differences simply leads to more and greater use of force? What if we realize that one species is capable of destroying all life on earth through the use of weapons that are beyond most people's imagination?

What if all educational organizations collectively said "We are going to dedicate all our efforts to the cause of peace?" Imagine CASE meetings dedicated to the subject of peace. CAAE would devote a conference to the cause of peace. Alumni directors would ask all alumni clubs, constituent societies, class reunions and continuing education programs to dedicate meetings to the cause of peace.

What if every university, college and school from kindergarten through graduate school taught peace not war?

What if alumni directors sparked the flame of peace by simply saying "Let's start it ourselves?" Imagine CAAE and CASE getting together and sponsoring a World Peace Conference, inviting all the other education associations to participate.

If the world only looks backward and explores our historical differences, we will never have peace. It is easy for Americans to say, "Those people have fought for a thousand years. You will never get them to stop." Yet most recently we have watched a political schism in our own country that has been reduced to name-calling, hateful verbal abuse and an outpouring of vitriolic character assassination, completely abandoning a discussion of issues and ideas.

We live in a world where nature has bestowed an abundance of life-sustaining resources. We seem bent on destroying the environment as well as ourselves. We seem reluctant to deal with such issues, afraid of alienating a political base or causing an economic problem, but what challenge measures up to the destruction of earth and the living creatures that share the earth's bounty?

There are experts on university campuses in every discipline known to man. Where are the professors of peace?

Maybe alumni directors should assume such a role. There is a profound difference between anti-war and pro-peace.

SOCRATES ONCE SAID, "PERHAPS THE GREATEST PHRASE IN ANY LANGUAGE IS "NOW IN CLOSING".

APOLOGIES

When I started this book, I used the word "Ramblings" as a working title. As I reread the final copy, I realize that it was an appropriate title. It does indeed roam all over, lacks any real organization and often repeats various themes. Socrates might have thought it would have been far better to follow his own method of asking questions instead of the arrogance of assuming that I knew some of the answers.

The book does serve as a personal reminder of how fortunate I was to spend my life in the field of alumni relations. To work for a great cause at an equally great university, to do so with alumni who care and with colleagues who are your best friends, constitutes the best of all jobs. It should not be called work, but privilege.

EPILOGUE

THE SOCRATIC METHOD
(SHORT VERSION)

SOCRATES, "YOU SAY THAT THIS WRITER, FORMANUS, IS A FOOL?"

HEINLENEUS, "FOOL SEEMS APPROPRIATE."

PREOLUS, "I THINK IT FITS WELL."

SOCRATES, "WOULD YOU AGREE THAT TO JUDGE A PERSON ONE MUST HAVE EXPERTISE?"

HEINLENEUS AND PREOLUS IN UNISON, "WE DO."

SOCRATES, "MAY I ASK WHICH OF YOU IS THE EXPERT ON BEING A FOOL?"

HEINLENEUS, "HE IS."

PREOLUS, "HE IS."

SOCRATES, "I AM COMPELLED TO AGREE WITH BOTH OF YOU."

SOCRATES 470-399 BCE

Socrates purportedly was a stonemason, his father's occupation. His education was that of a typical Athenian of his time. However, it has been rumored that he would have gone to the University of Michigan had he lived in another era.

Living heirs of Socrates have demanded a disclaimer for any quotes in this book attributed to him

ABOUT THE AUTHOR

ROBERT G. FORMAN
EXECUTIVE DIRECTOR EMERITUS
THE ALUMNI ASSOCIATION OF THE UNIVERSITY OF MICHIGAN

Forman received his BA from Michigan State University and his MPA from the University of Michigan.

He served the University of Michigan as executive director of the University Alumni Association for 28 years. During his tenure, the association was recognized as one of the premier alumni organizations in America.

The association pioneered programs in continuing education for alumni, recruitment of underrepresented minorities, alumni family camping, educational travel programs, continuing education for women and other programs of service to alumni and the university.

At the University of Michigan, he was selected as an honorary member of the Varsity M Club and a member of the senior honorary, Michigamua.

Forman was elected chairman of the Board of the Council for the Advancement and Support of Education (CASE) and was the founding president of the Council of Alumni Association Executives (CAAE). He was the first recipient of the Father Theodore Hesburgh Award for contributions to higher education. In 2006, he was awarded the Lifetime Achievement Award by CASE.

He has been honored by the creation of the Forman Fellows program, established by the CAAE, and the Robert G. Forman Scholarship Fund at the University of Michigan, created by the University of Michigan Alumni Association.

In retirement he has served as a consultant, speaker and author. He and his wife Patti share their retirement between their homes in northern Michigan and Florida.

Printed in the United States
86919LV00006B/172-177/A

9 781934 246689